Excel

YEARS 7 to 8

Reading and Vocabulary Workbook

ESSENTIAL skills

Get the Results You Want!

Maya Puiu

Reprinted 2017, 2020, 2022, 2025

ISBN 978 1 74125 408 2

Pascal Press
PO Box 250
Glebe NSW 2037
(02) 9198 1748
www.pascalpress.com.au

Publisher: Vivienne Joannou
Project editors: Mark Dixon and Leanne Poll
Edited by Leanne Howard
Series developer and consultant: Kristine Brown
Reviewed by Justine Hodgson
Cover and page design by DiZign Pty Ltd
Typeset by lj Design (Julianne Billington)
Printed by Vivar Printing/Green Giant Press

Contents

To the student

This book is designed to lead you through some essential reading skills as well as develop your vocabulary and language. Reading more, and thinking and writing about what you are reading, will develop your skills as an English student. First you will strengthen your reading comprehension skills; then you will develop your understanding of the language and literary techniques that writers use to achieve a particular purpose for a particular audience.

Each chapter is divided into six sections. The exercises and examples in each chapter relate as much as possible to the main reading text used in each chapter.

Before you read—*this section contains pre-reading activities designed to get you thinking about the text you are about to read and engage with.*

Test your understanding—*this section contains a range of comprehension questions that will test your understanding of the text you have just read.*

Boost your reading skills—*this section will focus on a particular reading skill, such as understanding main ideas and deducing the meaning of words.*

Work on words—*this section focuses on improving your vocabulary and understanding of words.*

Spotlight on language—*this section focuses on an aspect of language that is present in each chapter.*

Extend your skills—*this last question allows you to extend and develop the ideas presented in the chapter.*

Take your time when completing the exercises and think carefully about what skill each exercise is trying to teach you. This book will help you become a better reader and give you skills that you can use when reading new and different texts.

I wish you the best of luck and I hope you enjoy the activities.

Maya Puiu

UNIT ONE

Novel extract

Before you read

The **first paragraph** of any text is important as it provides key information about the content and the type of text you are about to read. This sets up your expectations about the remainder of the text and makes it easier for you to read and understand.

Read the **first paragraph** only and then circle the correct word for each summary.

1	The text is about a	boy.	girl.	kangaroo.	woman.
2	The text is set in	the country.	a made-up world.	the city.	
3	The text is an example of	comedy.	science fiction.	adventure.	

An extract from *Dot and the Kangaroo* by Ethel C Pedley

Chapter 1

Little Dot had lost her way in the bush. She knew it, and was very frightened. She was too frightened in fact to cry, but stood in the middle of a little dry, bare space, looking around her at the scraggy growths of prickly shrubs that had torn her little dress to rags, scratched her bare legs and feet till they bled, and pricked her hands and arms as she had pushed madly through the bushes, for hours, seeking her home. Sometimes she looked up to the sky. But little of it could be seen because of the great tall trees that seemed to her to be trying to reach heaven with their far-off crooked branches. She could see little patches of blue sky between the tangled tufts of the very drooping leaves, and, as the dazzling sunlight had faded, she began to think it was getting late, and that very soon it would be night.

The thought of being lost and alone in the wild bush at night, took her breath away with fear, and made her tired little legs tremble under her. She gave up all hope of finding her home, and sat down at the foot of the biggest Blackbutt tree, with her face buried in her hands and knees, and thought of all that had happened, and what might happen yet.

It seemed such a long, long time since her mother had told her that she might gather some bush flowers while she cooked the dinner, and Dot recollected how she was bid not to go out of sight of the cottage. How she wished now she had remembered this sooner! But whilst she was picking the pretty flowers, a hare suddenly started at her feet and sprang away into the bush, and she had run after it. When she found that she could not catch the hare, she discovered that she could no longer see the cottage. After wandering for a while she got frightened and ran, and ran, little knowing that she was going further away from her home at every step.

Where she was sitting under the blackbutt tree, she was miles away from her father's selection, and it would be very difficult for anyone to find her. She felt that she was a long way off, and she began to think of what was happening at home. She remembered how, not very long ago, a neighbour's little boy had been lost, and how his mother had come to their cottage for help to find him, and that her father had ridden off on the big bay horse to bring men from all the selections around to help in the search. She remembered their coming back in the darkness; numbers of strange men she had never seen before. Old men, young men, and boys, all on their rough-coated horses, and how they came indoors, and what a noise they made all talking together in their big deep voices. They looked terrible men, so tall and brown and fierce, with their rough bristly beards; and they all spoke in such funny tones to her, as if they were trying to make their voices small.

During many days, these men came and went, and every time they were more sad, and less noisy. The little boy's mother used to come and stay, crying, whilst the men were searching the bush for her little son. Then, one evening, Dot's father came home alone, and both her mother and the little boy's mother went away in a great hurry. Then, very late, her mother came back crying, and her father sat smoking by the fire looking very sad, and she never saw that little boy again, although he had been found.

She wondered now if all these rough, big men were riding into the bush to find her, and if, after many days, they would find her, and no one ever see her again. She seemed to see her mother crying, and her father very sad, and all the men very solemn. These thoughts made her so miserable that she began to cry herself.

Dot does not know how long she was sobbing in loneliness and fear, with her head on her knees, and with her little hands covering her eyes so as not to see the cruel wild bush in which she was lost. It seemed a long time before she summoned up courage to uncover her weeping eyes, and look once more at the bare, dry earth, and the wilderness of scrub and trees that seemed to close her in as if she were in a prison. When she did look up, she was surprised to see that she was no longer alone. She forgot all her trouble and fear in her astonishment at seeing a big grey Kangaroo squatting quite close to her, in front of her.

Source: http://gutenberg.net.au/ebooks09/0900681.txt

Test your understanding

1 Mark the following statements True (T) or False (F).

- **a** Dot is lost in the Australian bush. ______
- **b** Dot is unafraid and confident. ______
- **c** Dot chased a kangaroo into the bush. ______
- **d** The weather is clear and the sun is shining. ______
- **e** A large group of men are out looking for her. ______
- **f** Dot has been lost for 2 days. ______

2 In which order do these events occur? Number them 1 to 5.

- **a** ______ Dot remembers the time when her neighbour's son got lost.
- **b** ______ Dot suddenly realises there is a large kangaroo near her.
- **c** ______ The sun is fading and it will soon be night-time.
- **d** ______ Dot recalled when her mother asked her to collect some bush flowers.
- **e** ______ A group of large strange men come into her home.

3 Tick (✓) the correct answer. How did Dot get lost?

- **a** The dazzling sunlight caused her to lose her way. ______
- **b** She was collecting flowers. ______
- **c** She chased after a hare. ______
- **d** She was running away from home. ______

4 Tick (✓) the correct answer. Choose the sentence that best conveys Dot's feelings at being lost.

- **a** 'Little Dot had lost her way in the bush.' ______
- **b** 'The thought of being lost and alone … took her breath away with fear.' ______
- **c** 'How she wished now she had remembered this sooner!' ______
- **d** 'It seemed a long time before she summoned up courage to uncover her weeping eyes.' ______

5 Tick (✓) the correct answer. In paragraph 4, Dot recalls an incident where another child had been lost in the bush. What do you think is the writer's purpose in including this incident?

a Remembering a story about home comforts Dot. ______

b The story of the lost boy gives the audience hope that she will be found. ______

c The memory adds further fear and tension to Dot's situation. ______

d Dot has lots of time available to think about her past. ______

6 Using your own words, write why you think Dot was so surprised and amazed to see, at the end of the extract, a 'big grey Kangaroo squatting quite close to her'.

____

____

Boost your reading skills

Inferring to get an overall meaning

Inference is just a big word that describes what you do when you draw **conclusions** or use your **judgement**. If you infer that something has happened when reading, you do not necessarily read about the actual event. You use other information and your knowledge of the world to 'read between the lines'.

Writers often give you hints or clues that help you 'read between the lines'. When you infer, you go beyond the surface details to see other meanings that are suggested, hinted at or implied (not stated).

In making inferences you are really getting at the overall meaning of what you are reading: **what** is important, **why** it is important, and **how** events occur and lead on to other events.

Use your own knowledge and understanding of the world to infer overall meaning.

1 Look at these examples and write what you think each **infers**.

a A shadow passed over Lena's face when she opened her birthday present.

Inference: ______________________________

b I wouldn't eat on that table after that two year old if I were you.

Inference: ______________________________

c Simon wasn't allowed to come to the movies on Friday night.

Inference: ______________________________

d Later that day we had ice-cream cones, but they melted quickly.

Inference: ______________________________

e We had to move quickly to the left-hand lane and let the ambulance pass.

Inference: ______________________________

2 In the story excerpt 'Dot and the Kangaroo', Dot refers to an unpleasant memory of another missing child. The reader is not told directly what happened to the other child, and must use **inference** to understand what happened. Look on the next page at the examples from the text and answer the questions.

They looked terrible men, so tall and brown and fierce, with their rough bristly beards; and they all spoke in such funny tones to her, as if they were trying to make their voices small. (paragraph 4)

a Are the men known to Dot? How do you know? ______________________________

____

b What does *terrible* mean in this sentence? ______________________________

____

c Why are they trying to make their voices *small* when speaking to Dot? ______________

____

During many days, these men came and went, and every time they were more sad, and less noisy. (paragraph 5)

d Why are the men *more sad and less noisy* the more they come and go?

____

____

Her mother came back crying, and her father sat smoking by the fire looking very sad, and she never saw that little boy again, although he had been found. (paragraph 5)

e What has really happened to the little boy?

____

f How does Dot feel about this memory? Find a quote from the story to support your answer.

____

____

____

____

Work on words

Adjectives to create a descriptive setting

When you read, important descriptive information is provided by **adjectives**. It's essential to pay attention to these as they provide crucial details about what you are reading.

Adjectives **add details** to **nouns** and **pronouns**.

Adjectives are very often used in **descriptions of settings**. The setting is the situation or location in which a story or event occurs. Setting can include specific information about time and place and is usually highly descriptive. Physical location, historical information, social conditions, climate, immediate surroundings and time of day can all be aspects of setting.

The author creates the setting by providing information about time and place, and uses descriptive language, including adjectives, to effectively create vivid sights, sounds, smells and other sensations.

In the following examples, the highlighted words are **adjectives**.

- The **coarse** pebbles hurt her feet as she walked barefoot.
- The **old** lady washed her **bathroom** sink with a **used yellow** cloth.
- The attic is **dark** and **humid**.
- **Many** people have already begun to buy **shiny new school** shoes.

1 Look at the examples from the story and underline the **adjectives** you find. Then answer the question under each example. The first one has been done for you.

a 'She could see little patches of blue sky … as the dazzling sunlight had faded … soon it would be night.'

b What is the weather like?

The weather is clear and the sun was shining and strong. However, the day is getting late.

c 'She … stood in the middle of a little dry, bare space … looking around her at the straggly growths of prickly shrubs'

d What is the landscape/environment like?

e '… torn her little dress to rags.'

f How does the use of the adjective make the reader feel towards Dot?

g '… great tall trees that seemed to her to be trying to reach heaven with their far-off crooked branches.'

h Why is the height of the trees exaggerated here?

i 'She could see little patches of blue sky between the tangled tufts of the very drooping leaves.'

j How would only being able to see *little patches of blue sky* make Dot feel?

2 Using your own words, what **overall feeling/impression** about Dot's location does the opening paragraph give you?

3 Look at the following sentences from the story. They each use good, strong adjectives. Replace each underlined **adjective** with another suitable adjective from those provided by circling it. Use a dictionary if you need to look up the words.

a 'They looked terrible men, so tall and brown and <u>fierce</u>, with their rough bristly beards.'

fiery severe simple

b 'She wondered now if all these rough, <u>big</u> men were riding into the bush to find her …'

enormous great tall

c '… and look once more at the <u>bare</u>, dry earth and the wilderness of scrub and trees …'

glaring plain stark

4 Now replace the highlighted **adjectives** with your own best descriptive adjective.

a 'She was too frightened in fact to cry, but stood in the middle of a little **dry**, bare space, looking around her at the **scraggy** growths of prickly shrubs that had torn her little dress to rags …'

dry ______________________ scraggy ______________________

b '… with her head on her knees, and with her little hands covering her eyes so as not to see the **cruel wild** bush in which she was lost.'

cruel ______________________ wild ______________________

5 The writer often uses quite simple **adjectives** when describing Dot's experiences and feelings, such as *little*, *dry*, *bare* and *big*. Based on what you know about Dot, can you provide a reason why the author may have done this?

____

____

____

____

Spotlight on language

A narrative perspective

Narrative writing is always told from someone's **point of view**. This point of view is the perspective from which characters and events are presented by the **narrator** or **'voice'** of the narrative.

The point of view chosen can have a strong effect on the reader.

An author can choose to have either a first-person or a third-person narrator for a story.

First-person narrator: the narrator is a character in the story and uses the first-person singular (*I*) or first-person plural (*we*). The reader tends to identify with the narrator.

For example: I do not know how long I was sobbing in loneliness and fear.

Third-person narrator: the narrator stands outside the story and uses the third person (*he*, *she* or *they*, or *by name*) to refer to the characters. The reader can see things the characters cannot see, and has a wider view of events.

For example: Dot does not know how long she was sobbing in loneliness and fear.

1 Read these short extracts from well-known stories. In the space provided, write *FP* if it is a **first-person** narrative or *TP* if it is a **third-person** narrative.

a ______ Scrooge knew he was dead? Of course he did. How could it be otherwise? Scrooge and he were partners for many years. (Charles Dickens, *A Christmas Carol*)

b ______ The thousand injuries of Fortunato I had borne as best as I could; but when he ventured upon insult, I vowed revenge. (Edgar Allan Poe, 'The Cask of Amontillado') ______________________________

c ______ One evening recently, the lady whom Uncle Remus calls "Miss Sally" missed her little seven-year-old. (*Brer Rabbit and the Tar-Baby* by Joel Chandler Harris)

____

d ______ When we started for our drive the sun was shining brightly on Munich, and the air was full of the joyousness of early summer. (*Dracula's Guest* by Bram Stoker)

____

e ______ Whether I shall turn out to be the hero of my own life or whether that station will be held by anybody else, these pages must show. (Charles Dickens, *David Copperfield*) ______________________________

f ______ The gaunt man with the scarred lip was the first to speak. "Nowhere", he said, with a sigh of disappointment in his voice. (*The Valley of Spiders* by H. G. Wells)

____

2 The following examples are from 'Dot and the Kangaroo', which is written in the third-person point-of-view. Change each example to the **first person**. Clues have been given for the first three examples. The first one has been done for you.

a Little Dot had lost her way in the bush. She knew it, and was very frightened.

I had lost my way in the bush. I knew it, and was very frightened.

b It seemed such a long, long time since her mother had told her that she might gather some bush flowers while she cooked the dinner.

____

____

c She wondered now if all these rough, big men were riding into the bush to find her, and if, after many days, they would find her and no one ever see her again.

____

____

d She seemed to see her mother crying, and her father very sad, and all the men very solemn.

____

____

e It seemed a long time before she summoned up courage to uncover her weeping eyes, and look once more at the bare, dry earth.

____

____

Extend your skills

Reread the final paragraph of the story. What do you think happens to Dot next? Continue the story for another paragraph. Try to continue the style of the original story—this means you should write using the **third-person narrator** and use the same kind of language, sentence lengths and punctuation that the original author has.

UNIT TWO

Web article

Before you read

It is always easier to understand what you are reading if you have some **background knowledge** and **experience** of the topic. Activating this knowledge and experience helps you make connections between new and known information.

1 When is Australia Day? ______________________________

____

2 How do you celebrate Australia Day?

____

____

____

3 How do you think Australians living overseas might celebrate Australia Day?

____

____

____

How to celebrate Australia Day

Jane Roseen

How to celebrate Australia Day

Food Articles | January 8, 2006

Join in the festivities and celebrate Australia Day, even if you aren't in Australia! Throw an Australia Day party, complete with chocolate, in the true spirit of Australian 'mateship'—friendly companionship with many different people.

For those outside of the Southern Hemisphere who wish to celebrate Australia Day, it can seem somewhat difficult to do so in an authentic manner. As January 26 falls during the heat of the Australian summer, people like to celebrate with outdoorsy activities. But the chill of the winter for those of us north of the equator can dampen this sun-loving spirit. No matter! You too can celebrate Australia Day from the Northern Hemisphere!

For those interested in as authentic an experience as possible, check your local paper. Some large cities offer organised activities for Australia Day, allowing both locals and Australian expatriates to celebrate together. These activities can be a great way to learn more about Australia Day, as well as give you a place where you can have loads of fun with people from all over the world.

If a large crowd doesn't appeal to you or you don't have any organised Australia Day activities in your area, it's your turn to throw an Australia Day party instead! The spirit of Australia, after all, is known to be that of 'mateship'—friendly companionship with many different people. Your friends and family will love the opportunity to gather and maybe learn while still enjoying a winter barbecue. Yes, a winter barbecue. Sounds like a complete oxymoron, but you can make it a party they'll not soon forget! Decorate the interior of your home with classic barbecue accessories like party lanterns, tropical plants and picnic areas. Use lots of lights to come as close to a bright summer day as possible and complement your theme.

For food, find foods that can be prepared without a grill while still lending an authentic barbecue flair. A great option would be some form of a kebab—either meat-loving or vegetarian will do. These can be baked in the oven but still scream 'barbecue!' To lend even more of an Australian flair, offer a variety of sauces for your guests to try. Australia's culture is so diverse that many different genres can be covered. Maybe a peanut sauce, a mole sauce (pronounced 'mo-lay', a combination of chocolate and peanuts), a ginger sauce, a classic barbeque sauce ... the possibilities are limitless!

For dessert, think of the desserts that bring a barbecue to a tasty close. If you can find fresh fruit of good quality, combining that with angel food cake on a platter surrounded by small chocolate wafers offers your guests a variety of sweets from which to choose. Or maybe a great way to warm up the crowd before they venture back out into the cold would be a bit less traditional for barbecues—offer plates with several varieties of biscotti and then create customised coffee drinks.

Regardless of where you are, you can celebrate Australia Day with your family and friends. These celebrations are sure to bring a bright spot of warmth and joy to your otherwise dreary January chill.

Source: Free Articles from ArticlesFactory.com

Test your understanding

1 Mark the following statements True (T) or False (F).

- **a** Australia Day is celebrated on January 26. ______
- **b** The article encourages people to celebrate Australia Day. ______
- **c** The article is mainly about outdoor activities. ______
- **d** The article is aimed at people who want to visit Australia. ______
- **e** The article suggests that celebrating with others will enhance your barbecue. ______
- **f** Check your local paper to find ideas for celebrating in your area. ______

2 Tick (✓) the correct answer. Who is this article written for?

- **a** all Australians ______
- **b** people outside the Southern Hemisphere ______
- **c** Australians living in the Northern Hemisphere ______
- **d** people wishing to live like Australians ______

3 Tick (✓) the correct answer. What is the article's main topic or theme?

- **a** barbecues ______
- **b** food ______
- **c** holidays ______
- **d** desserts ______

4 What is the evidence for your answer to Question 3?

____

____

____

____

____

____

____

____

5 Tick (✓) the correct answer. In the sentence 'But the chill of the winter for those of us north of the equator can dampen this sun-loving spirit', what does *dampen* mean?

a increase ______

b strengthen ______

c diminish ______

d irritate ______

6 Tick (✓) the correct answer. The article describes *mateship* (paragraph 4) as

a social and pleasant friendship with lots of different people. ______

b looking after your friends. ______

c cooking your friends a barbecue meal. ______

d being kind to many different people. ______

7 Tick (✓) the correct answer. In the sentence, 'For those outside of the Southern Hemisphere who wish to celebrate Australia Day, it can seem somewhat difficult to do so in an authentic manner', the word *authentic* could be replaced with

a faithful. ______

b dependable. ______

c reliable. ______

d realistic. ______

8 Use your own words to describe this line from paragraph 6: 'Kebabs … can be baked in the oven, but still scream "barbeque!"'

____

____

____

____

____

____

____

____

Boost your reading skills

Understanding main ideas

Many students have trouble **recognising main ideas** in texts. In order to understand and demonstrate the main idea of a paragraph, you must not only understand what you are reading but also **make connections within the text**. The process of identifying main ideas involves locating non-essential and unimportant ideas in order to 'eliminate' information that does not contribute to the main idea.

The **first paragraph** of what you are reading usually provides a good **summary** of the main idea of the text. After that, the main place to find main ideas is in the **opening sentence** of each paragraph. For this reason, the opening sentence is often called the **topic sentence**.

Finding the main idea helps you:

- **understand** the writer's message
- **tell** someone about a text without having to tell them everything
- **concentrate** on important parts of the text
- **write** a summary and remember information.

1 Write your own definition of the term *the main idea*. What does it mean to you?

____

____

____

____

____

____

____

2 In the article, information about things that happen—who, what, where, when and why—are important **clues** to understanding the main ideas. Answer these questions to help you find the article's **main ideas**.

a Who is the article about?

____

b What is the article about?

____

c What locations (where) is the article concerned with?

____

d When was the article written?

____

e Why was the article written?

____

Summarising means writing ideas using your own words and in a shorter form than the original text. Understanding main ideas will make you a better summariser.

3 Look at the opening paragraph from the Australia Day article. Reread it and then fill in the blanks to create its **summary**.

Join in the festivities and celebrate Australia Day, even if you aren't in Australia! Throw an Australia Day party, complete with chocolate, in the true spirit of Australian 'mateship'—friendly companionship with many different people.

Even if you aren't in ____________________, you could throw an 'Australia Day' ________.

Celebrating with many different ____________ shows the true meaning of '____________________'.

Creating a **title** for **paragraphs** within an article is an effective way to show your understanding of that paragraph's main idea.

4 Start by underlining the **key words** (most important words) in each paragraph, then think of a title for each paragraph that shows the **main idea** of that paragraph. The first one has been done for you.

a For those outside of the Southern Hemisphere who wish to celebrate Australia Day, it can seem somewhat difficult to do so in an authentic manner. As January 26 falls during the heat of the Australian summer, people like to celebrate with outdoorsy activities. But the chill of the winter for those of us north of the equator can dampen this sun-loving spirit. No matter! You too can celebrate Australia Day from the Northern Hemisphere!

Paragraph title: Celebrating Australia Day in the Northern Hemisphere

b For those interested in as authentic an experience as possible, check your local paper. Some large cities offer organised activities for Australia Day, allowing both locals and Australian ex-patriots to celebrate together. These activities can be a great way to learn more about Australia Day, as well as give you a place where you can have loads of fun with people from all over the world.

Paragraph title: ____

c For dessert, think of the desserts that bring a barbecue to a tasty close. If you can find fresh fruit of good quality, combining that with angel food cake on a platter surrounded by small chocolate wafers offers your guests a variety of sweets from which to choose. Or maybe a great way to warm up the crowd before they venture back out into the cold would be a bit less traditional for barbecues—offer plates with several varieties of biscotti and then create customised coffee drinks.

Paragraph title: ____

Work on words

Using the right word

Some words cause misunderstandings because they sound similar to other words. Words that sound the same but are spelt differently are called **homonyms**.

For example: words like *fair* and *fare* sound the same but have very different meanings.

At other times, words that are confusing are **spelt slightly differently** and have **slightly different pronunciations**.

For example: *desert* and *dessert*

1 Read the following examples from the *Australia Day* article and circle the correct word. Then complete the sentence.

a Join in the festivities and celebrate Australia Day, even if you (aren't/aunt) in Australia!

Use the correct word (aunt/aren't) to complete these sentences.

- **i** When is your ________________ coming to visit?
- **ii** You ________________ leaving tomorrow, are you?
- **iii** ________________ you and your ________________ coming to the end of year party?

b (Your/you're) friends and family will love the opportunity to gather and maybe learn while still enjoying a winter barbecue.

Use the correct word (your/you're) to complete these sentences.

- **i** '________________ coming whether or not you want to,' said Imran's mother.
- **ii** Where did you leave ________________ keys? I hope you find them!
- **iii** You never know where ________________ glasses are even though ________________ always looking for them.

c Use lots of lights to come as close to a bright summer day as possible and (complement/compliment) your theme.

Use the correct word (complement/compliment) to complete these sentences. Look them up in a dictionary if you need to.

- **i** It was so nice of you to ________________ me on my new haircut!
- **ii** I think a blue headband would ________________ your dress nicely.
- **iii** It would be a ________________ to your host if you made sure that the drink you bring will ________________ the food they serve.

d For food, find foods that can be prepared without a grill while still lending an authentic barbecue (flair/flare).

Use the correct word (flair/flare) to complete these sentences. Look them up in a dictionary if you need to.

- **i** My grandmother always dressed well and had her own unique ________________.
- **ii** The emergency ________________ forcefully shot into the sky.
- **iii** The fireworks technician showed real ________________ when he timed the lighting of the final multicoloured ________________.

e If you can find fresh fruit of good quality, combining that with (angle/angel) food cake on a platter surrounded by small chocolate wafers offers your guests a variety of (suites/sweets) from which to (choose/chews).

Use the correct word (angle/angel, suites/sweets or choose/chews) to complete these sentences. Look them up in a dictionary if you need to.

- **i** The tradesperson measured the ________________ of the wall to make sure the cupboard would fit.
- **ii** Mum said I was a little ________________ for all the help I gave her in preparing for dinner.
- **iii** I'm not allowed to eat any ________________ until I finish my main meal.
- **iv** In the hotel, there were a variety of one- and two-bedroom ____________ to choose from.
- **v** The cow ________________ grass slowly and ponderously.
- **vi** I wondered which pair of glasses I would ________________.

2 Here are some other examples of words that are commonly confused.

desert—a noun/adjective meaning 'a very dry, arid place'
desert—a verb meaning 'leave or run away'
dessert—a noun for the sweet course that is served after a main meal

a Use one of these words to complete the sentences.

i The soldier was afraid to ________________ as he knew he would get into trouble.

ii I really hope we have apple pie and cream tonight for ________________.

iii The camel plodded slowly through the extreme heat of the ________________, searching for water.

iv In the ________________, it's impossible to have ice-cream for ________________ because it's so hot!

allowed—past tense and past participle of the verb *allow*
aloud—adverb meaning 'say something so that you can be heard'

b Use one of these words to complete the sentences.

i I really hope I will be ________________ to visit the museum this weekend with my best friend!

ii When the baby is sleeping, it's important not to speak ________________ in case we wake him.

iii I was ________________ to read ________________ to the kindergarten students last week—it was very exciting.

bare—adjective meaning 'uncovered or exposed'
bear—noun for an animal or verb to describe something you are carrying or holding up

c Use one of these words to complete the sentences.

i The sun beat down on her ________________ head, causing her to burn.

ii We visited the zoo for the sole purpose of viewing a real ________________.

iii The box was a heavy burden to ________________ and made him tire quickly.

iv The ________________ landscape was treeless, dry and uninhabitable.

v The ________________ was ________________ as he was old and had lost his fur.

3 Write a sentence that includes the following words. The first one has been done for you.

a dessert, you're

You're only going to be given dessert if you have eaten all the salad on your plate.

b your, flare

____

____

c desert, bare

____

____

____

d aloud, compliment

____

____

____

e bear, chews

____

____

____

f aunt, complement

____

____

____

Spotlight on language

Oxymorons

An **oxymoron** is a literary term that puts together two contradictory (opposite) terms or ideas. Even the word *oxymoron* is an oxymoron, because it comes from combining the Greek words for sharp (*oxy*) and dull (*moros*).

Some common examples of oxymorons are:

* working holiday—holidays are not about completing work
* small crowd—a crowd is a large group
* exact estimate—an estimate is never exact
* peacekeeping force—a force implies war and aggression and is not peaceful
* silent scream—scream means 'cry aloud'
* genuine imitation—an imitation is never genuine
* living dead—it's impossible to be living and dead
* same difference—a difference is never the same as anything else.

Sometimes an oxymoron is used to **highlight** an **idea** for the reader or listener, and sometimes it is used to make the audience pause and think, to make them laugh and to make them consider the ideas being presented.

For example: The *Australia Day* article at the start of the unit uses the word *oxymoron* to highlight a point or an idea about having a winter barbecue.

Yes, a **winter barbeque**. Sounds like a complete **oxymoron**, but you can make it a party they'll not soon forget! (Paragraph 5)

As we normally associate barbecues with summer in Australia, the author is highlighting the oddity or strangeness of having a barbeque in the Northern Hemisphere, which is experiencing winter when we celebrate Australia Day.

1 Match the words in each column to create your own **oxymoron**. The first one has been done for you.

bad	abrasive
natural	feeling
numb	luck
mild	order
fairly	fun
random	giant
serious	dark
little	aware
vaguely	additives

2 The following are famous quotes and expressions that contain examples of **oxymorons**. Underline the opposite or contradictory ideas. The first one has been done for you.

a A little pain never hurt anyone.

b 'Gentlemen, I want you to know that I am not always right, but I am never wrong.' Samuel Goldwyn

c Honk if you're against noise pollution!

d 'I'll give you a definite maybe.' Samuel Goldwyn

e 'I am a deeply superficial person.' Andy Warhol

f I'm proud of my humility.

g 'If I could drop dead right now, I'd be the happiest man alive!' Samuel Goldwyn

h 'If you fall and break your legs, don't come running to me.' Samuel Goldwyn

i 'Parting is such sweet sorrow.' William Shakespeare

j 'I distinctly remember forgetting that.' Clara Barton

3 Use your own words to explain the following examples of **oxymoron**.

a stand down ____

____

b true story ____

____

c loose tights ____

____

d taped live ____

____

e sure bet ____

Extend your skills

Write a **blog comment** in response to this article. You should provide some opinion about the article and whether you thought it offered good advice for celebrating Australia Day. Here is an example.

http://www.blog.com.au

HOME | CATEGORIES | ARCHIVES | FOOD RECEIPES | CONTACT US

Tim

Location: Canada October 13, 2012, 3:01PM

Great article—thanks for reminding all us Aussies (and anyone else!) who are overseas not to forget to celebrate Australia Day. I really liked the tips for creating a barbecue-like feel for your party, despite being in the cold of winter! Ahh, makes me long for the long hot summer of home. Just one issue—I've never heard of some of your sauces. What is a mole sauce? I'm pretty certain that's not an authentic Australian sauce. Shame also you didn't include some multicultural food or activities—we're not all barbecue lovers, you know!

UNIT THREE

Website advertisement

Before you read

Thinking about what you know of the text topic before and as you start reading a text will help you connect with the **information** and **ideas** it contains.

Quickly glance at the text below and then answer the questions.

1 Have you ever studied gymnastics?

2 What is your opinion of a gymnastics class aimed at children aged 2 to 5?

3 Imagine that some friends have asked you to use the web to help them find an exercise program for their preschool children. Look quickly at the advertisement below. Would you be likely to search further to find out what this organisation offers? Give your reasons.

Toddler Tumbles

Home **Our Programs** **About Us** **Contact Us** **FAQS**

Our Programs: Tumble Bugs, Tumble Bears, Tumble Tigers

About Us: Benefits, Coaches

Contact Us: Location, Bookings, Holiday Camps, Parties

Gymnastics for kids 2 to 5

CALL TO BOOK: (02) 9304 5070

Gymnastics is a fun, engaging approach to teaching children self-esteern and helping their growing bodies develop the strength and co-ordination that is vital for healthy lives. Toddler Tumbles kids gymnastics classes are developed to a weekly lesson plan that builds foundation gymnastics skills and allows children and carers to observe the progress being made from one week to the next. Classes are non-competitive and age-specific creating an environment that allows children's self-confidence to grow along with their physical ability.

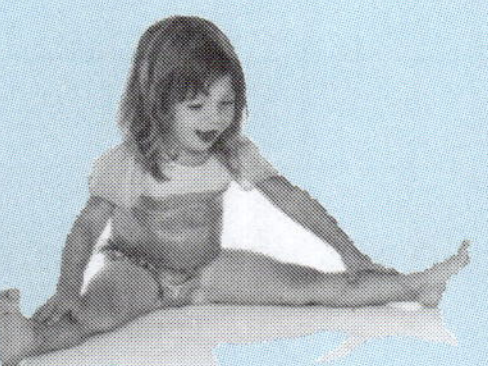

Tumble Bugs are our beginner 2-3 year olds. The use of bright colours, fun songs and carer participation allows children to engage easily and fully with the kids gymnastics class.

Tumble Bears are our intermediate 3-4 year olds. Tumble Bears are able to extend their core gymnastics skills to more challenging kids gymnastics activities.

Tumble Tigers are our advanced 4-5 year olds. Tumble Tiger kids gymnastics classes are more structured and carried out without carers, encouraging independence and self confidence.

Term 2 2012 begins Monday 30th April.

Call now to book your place in our fantastic kids gymnastics class!

Monday or Friday

Tumble Bugs: 9:30am to 10:10 am
Tumble Bears: 10:15am to 11:00 am
Tumble Tigers: 11:10am to 12:00 pm

Test your understanding

1 Mark the following statements True (T) or False (F).

a There are three levels of gymnastics available. ______
b The classes are for children aged 2 to 8. ______
c Children compete with one another for prizes. ______
d Tumble Tigers are for the older children. ______
e Classes occur every Monday and Wednesday. ______
f Tumble Bugs classes have fun songs. ______

2 Tick (✓) the correct answer. What is the purpose of this advertisement?

a to inform ______
b to instruct and explain ______
c to persuade ______
d to persuade and inform ______

3 Tick (✓) the correct answer. Who do you think this website is aimed at?

a children ______
b gymnasts ______
c parents and carers of children aged 2 to 5 years old ______
d preschool teachers ______

4 Tick (✓) the correct answer. The picture of the little figure in the top left corner is known as a *logo*. What is its purpose?

a to be entertaining for readers ______
b to provide information about the program ______
c to appeal to young children ______
d to make it easy for people to recognise *Toddler Tumbles* ______

5 A feature of Tumble Bugs is that there is *carer participation*. What do you think this means?

____

____

6 Tick (✓) the correct answer. We also learn that classes are non-competitive and *age-specific*. What does *age-specific* mean?

a Children aged 2 and 4 learn gymnastics together. ______

b Younger brothers and sisters are allowed to join in. ______

c Classes are organised for precise and definite age groups. ______

d The classes are a mix of all ages. ______

7 Tick (✓) the correct answer. What language technique is used in the business name *Toddler Tumbles*?

a rhyme (e.g. the red shed) ______

b simile (e.g. she was as fast as a leopard) ______

c assonance (e.g. a blue mood) ______

d alliteration (e.g. lick lemon lollipops) ______

8 The original webpage features a blue and orange colour scheme. Why do you think the advertisers have chosen blue and orange to promote their business?

____

____

____

9 Tick (✓) the correct answer. Which word could replace the word *vital* in the sentence: 'Gymnastics is … helping their growing bodies develop the strength and co-ordination that is *vital* for healthy lives'?

a essential

b unusual

c apparent

d good

10 Tick (✓) the correct answer. Look at the menus available in the webpage. Where would you expect to find information about securing a spot in a class for a child?

a Our programs

b Contact us

c Home

d FAQs

11 Thinking again about the friends who are looking for a class for their preschoolers, would you recommend Toddler Tumbles? Why or why not?

____

____

____

____

Boost your reading skills

Understanding the writer's purpose

All texts are created for a **purpose**. The table below contains some common purposes and text examples.

Some texts have more than one purpose. The text may use different language depending on the ideas it is trying to share with you. Think about the Toddler Tumbles advertisement. It is trying to sell you something (a service) as well as tell you about the service. This means that the advertisement has the purposes to **persuade** and to **inform**.

1 Can you think of any other text examples for each **purpose**?

Text purpose	Other examples
a instruct (e.g. computer manuals)	
b explain (e.g. online encyclopaedias, fact sheets)	
c entertain (e.g. novels, cartoons)	
d recount (e.g. diary)	
e persuade (e.g. advertisements, letters to the editor, political speeches)	
f inform (e.g. newspaper reports)	
g raise awareness (e.g. brochures, pamphlets, some advertising)	

2 Have a look at the following sentences. Label each with one **purpose** from the list above.

a Buy now! Limited stock on the amazing bagless vacuum cleaner from Sweden!

____

b Secondly, empty the contents of the red packet into a large bowl and stir in 250 mL of milk.

____

c It was a gloomy and foggy evening until, like a mirage, the moon emerged from nowhere.

____

d Today was a great day. I don't know why I feel so happy … I just hope the feeling lasts forever!

____

e Recycling is essential to help in the reduction of landfill waste. Please recycle correctly today.

____

f A fire broke out at 10 pm last night at the premises on Newhart Road. There were no casualties.

____

Informative language is usually factual and objective, while persuasive language uses descriptive adjectives and emotive language that is often colourful in order to gain an emotional reaction.

3 Group the following examples of language from the advertisement under the correct heading.

Tumble Bears are able to extend their core gymnastics skills
gymnastics is a fun, engaging approach
Tumble Bugs are our beginner 2-3 year olds
Tumble Tiger classes are more structured and carried out without carers
bright colours
NEW Fantastic gymnastics!

Language that persuades	**Language that informs**

4 Can you find any other examples of **informative** or **persuasive** language in the ad? List them as well.

______

______

______

Work on words

Latin prefixes

Latin was the official language of the Roman Empire. Local European languages were expanded by the addition of Latin terms when the Romans conquered parts of Europe, including England. As a result, many Latin words, Latin expressions and Latin roots are used in English.

Many words have **Latin prefixes**. A **prefix** is a letter or group of letters attached to the beginning of a word that changes the meaning of the root word.

1 The Latin **prefixes** *con, co, col, com* and *cor* mean 'with' or 'together' in many English words. Match the following words to their correct meaning by drawing a line to connect them.

collaborate	connect, link, associate
compress	behave with sympathy and kindness
correlate	gather together as a group or flock
congregate	cooperate, work together
compassion	press down on, to press together

2 Find three words from the *Toddler Tumbles* advertisment that contain the following **prefixes** and write the definition of each word.

a *co* ______ **Definition:** ______

b *com* ______________________ **Definition:** ______________________

c *con* ______________________ **Definition:** ______________________

3 **a** The Latin **prefix** *pro* means 'before', 'in front of', 'for' or 'forward'.

Match the following words to their correct meaning by drawing a line to connect them.

i prognosis	passage before the main part
ii propel	prediction of what will happen; a diagnosis
iii prophet	to act before, in advance
iv prologue	person who foretells the future
v proactive	forward motion

b The word *progress* appears in the advertisement. Does its **meaning** follow the example above (e.g. *pro* means 'before', 'in front of', 'for', or 'forward')?
Why/why not? Give reasons for your answer.

____

____

____

4 Each set of words on the right below share a prefix. Match each set to the meaning of the **prefix** on the left. The first one has been done for you.

Definitions	**Prefix examples**
a far, distant	unpopular, unkind, unhappy, unlucky
b eight	biweekly, bimonthly, biannual
c badly, wrong, incorrect	delete, deforestation, decentralise, decongest
d remove, take away, get rid of	television, telephone, telescope, telecommunication
e not (opposite of something)	reply, repeat, resend, restart, reboot, remember
f again, once more or back	preview, predict, prehistoric, prefix, preparation
g twice	octopus, octave, octogenarian, October
h one, whole, same	uniform, unify
i before	subway, submarine, subtract, subdue, subordinates
j under or low	mistake, misunderstand, misbehave, misread, miscalculate
k many or more than two	multiple, multiply, multicoloured, multilingual

Spotlight on language

Comparative adjectives in advertising

Most advertisements make frequent use of **adjectives** (describing words) to persuade people to buy their products.

For example: the advertisement uses *engaging, bright* and *weekly*.

Advertisers also use the comparative and superlative form of adjectives to make their product appear better by comparison, in order to persuade buyers to purchase what they are selling. They also use them to make comparisons between their product lines.

To make **comparative** or **superlative** adjectives, we add *er* or *est* to a simple adjective.

For example: bright (simple), brigh**ter** (comparative), brigh**test** (superlative).

Some comparative/superlative terms use the words *more* and *most*.

For example: beautiful, **more** beautiful, **most** beautiful.

The Toddler Tumbler web advertisement uses two examples of comparative adjectives.

1 Tumble Tigers kids gymnastics classes are **more structured**.

This sentence suggests that the classes are more structured and organised than the younger kids' gymnastic classes.

2 Tumble Bears are able to extend their core gymnastic skills to **more challenging** kids' gymnastics.

This sentence suggests that Tumble Bears will be more challenged than they will be in the younger kids' gymnastic classes.

1 Look at the following advertising statements. Fill in the blanks with a suitable **comparative adjective**. The first one has been done for you.

- **a** Brown's Boots are ___stronger___ than an Olympic weightlifter.
- **b** Molly's Muffins are ______________ than our rivals.
- **c** Mountain Fresh Water is ______________ than spring water from the Swiss Alps.
- **d** If you drink Harold's fresh juice you will be ______________________.
- **e** You will find our car is more ______________ than our competitor's.

The advertiser's **choice** of adjectives and comparative language can affect whether we as buyers believe what the advert is saying. If the comparative adjective is too extreme, then it is likely that the buyer will have a hard time trusting that the product can actually do what it says it can.

2 Have a look at the following examples of **comparative** and **superlative adjectives** used in advertising. Place a cross (✗) next to the underlined examples you feel are exaggerated and unbelievable. Place a tick (✓) next to the underlined examples you feel are acceptable. The first one has been done for you.

- **a** Our car will take you further than any other car on the market. ___✗___
- **b** The 'Snow Cone' is the iciest ice-cream available! ______
- **c** Our dictionary will allow you to find answers faster than any other dictionary. ______
- **d** 'Snuggie'—a more gentle washing powder for your baby. ______

e For hair that is shinier than your best friend's, use 'Shine-a-lot'. ______

f Our clothes dryer will have your towels drier than any of our competitors! ______

Extend your skills

In what ways does the advertisement try to **persuade** the reader to choose their gymnastic program? Consider layout, language and graphics.

In what ways are the placement and positioning of the different parts/sections of the advertisement (e.g. images, titles, paragraphs) effective? Is it easy for readers to locate different information and ideas?

What special language is used to persuade the audience to try Toddler Tumbles? Provide examples.

How are images and pictures used to enhance the advertisement? Explain the effect of each example.

UNIT FOUR

Interview

Before you read

Making predictions is more than just guessing what is going to happen next—it helps you become **actively involved** while you read a text and helps you remember information for longer.

1 Tick (✓) the correct answer. Look at the heading and then read the first four **bold** interview questions only—not the answers, just the questions.

This interview will mainly be about

a ______ a place called Wintersmith.

b ______ a book series called *Discworld*.

c ______ the author Terry Pratchett's books.

d ______ the author Terry Pratchett's favourite books.

2 Now read all the questions as a further previewing activity.

Interview with author Terry Pratchett

1 For people who haven't read the *Discworld* books, how would you explain the Discworld?

I'm not very good at it, but other people have said it's fantasy for people who don't like fantasy, it's like *Lord Of The Rings*, 500 years on when everyone's settled down a bit and everyone's trying to make an honest buck.

It's a parody of fantasy and parodies of the real world, and humorous fantasy—it's all those things.

2 You do have a lot of recurring characters you have Death, and the Librarian ...

Especially a very popular character! People keep writing to me, "Can we have more Death in this book?"

3 Do you have any favourite characters at all?

For an author, the nice characters aren't much fun. What you want are the screwed up characters. You know the characters that are constantly wondering if what they are doing is the right thing, characters that are not only screwed up but are self-tapping screws. They're doing it for themselves.

Commander Vimes of the City Watch, he's one of them, and there's Granny Weatherwax, a very senior witch, she's another one ... and they make interesting people because they become real. Because we're all a bit screwed up, unfortunately, it's the 21st Century, it's what happens.

4 Your latest book is *Wintersmith* which follows on the story of Tiffany Aching. Tell us a little about that.

The thing is, *Discworld* had been going on for a very long time and I've written children's books as well. Usually when people have a really big series they franchise it, which I thought is a bit of a no-no, so I thought what I'd do is I'd franchise it to myself.

So, in addition to doing the adult *Discworld* books, I thought I'd do a children's series with slightly changed characters and different places but it would still be *Discworld*.

Then I did the *Tiffany Aching* series—Mostly I did it because it annoyed me that all fairies and goblins always seemed to be English. I thought it would make them far more funny if they were all Scottish.

Basically they are all like Billy Connolly but about six inches high and slightly worse if possible. I'm sure everyone in Australia has seen Billy Connolly.

They befriend this young girl called Tiffany Aching; she's very good at making cheese. She's nine years old when she meets them and she wants to be a witch for all kinds of complicated reasons and they both help and hinder her during her career because they're very very loyal and they're often very drunk. They have magic powers—they can get in and out of anywhere except pubs.

For people who haven't read the books they are the Mac Nac Feegles. *Wintersmith* is the third book—there is going to be four books about Tiffany Aching and the Mac Nac Feegles or the Wee Free Men as they're called.

5 There's a bit of a rumour going around that there is going to be a film based on the *wee free men*.

Sam Rami who is the director of Spiderman, is going to make it for Sony.

6 How did you start writing?

I just did. There's no magical holy grail. There is no mystical map or anything like that.

One thing that writers have in common is that they are readers first. They have read lots and lots of stuff, because they're just infested with lots of stuff. If you are going to write, say, fantasy—stop reading fantasy. You've already read too much. Read other things; read westerns, read history, read anything that seems interesting, because if you only read fantasy and then you start to write fantasy, all you're going to do is recycle the same old stuff and move it around a bit. The next thing you know you've got a dark lord and there is no help for you.

You have to have really wide reading habits and pay attention to the news and just everything that's going on in the world: you need to. If you get this right then the writing is a piece of cake.

7 I think that answers my next question—which is what advice would you give to new writers or young writers?

Well please don't send your manuscript to me because I don't read them anymore. It gets very dangerous for an established author to read unpublished manuscripts just in case someone says "hey you stole my idea"!

In all seriousness, people think that it's the ideas that are important, well everyone has ideas, all the time, I tend to write mine down and remember them, but at some point you have to apply the bum to the seat and knock out about sixty-five thousand words, that's how long a novel is. You actually have to do all this and you have to let spelling and punctuation and grammar enter your life.

8 So what do people care about in books? What makes a good book do you think?

If you get the characters right you've done sometimes nearly half the work. I sometimes find I get the characters right then the characters will often help me write the book—not what they look like, that's not very important—what people look like is not about their character. You have to describe the shape they leave in the world, how they react to things, what effect they have on people and you do that by telling their story.

You don't write down "he was quite tall he had long hair and blue eyes", that isn't very descriptive, that's just a photograph.

You can work on a character to get them nicely rounded as if they are a real person. Get that right and you're doing extremely well.

9 What's your favourite band?

All-time favourite is the Steeleye Span who are one of the earliest folk rock groups.

10 Now this is a very trick question: chips or chocolate?

Um, I suppose chocolate and chips are out of the question, only one or the other? Any true aficionado would go for both. Actually ... chocolate.

11 If you had to be an amusement park ride which one would you be and why?

Oh it would definitely be the haunted house; you could have such a lot of fun in the dark. Whoooooooooooo!

12 What would you use as the first line as a thread on a message board?

I think it's widely agreed that the words "it was a dark and stormy night" are often a very good way of starting out. But one of the best introductions ever—I think someone actually did this in a book, to be a writer, you really have to get that audience's attention right at the start and so it was—"Dead, that's what he was when the police found him".

13 And finally what question would you like to ask the Rollercoastrians?

Can anyone tell me what *it's* all about because I'm 58 years old and I haven't found out what it's all about yet.

answer this question on RollerChat »

Test your understanding

1 Mark the following statements True (T) or False (F).

a Terry Pratchett is an author. ______

b Terry writes romance novels. ______

c A film is going to be made about the *Wee Free Men.* ______

d Terry believes that to be a good writer, you need to read a lot of everything. ______

e The 'nice' characters are the best to write about. ______

2 Tick (✓) the correct answer. In section 1, Terry says about his book: 'It's a parody of fantasy and parodies of the real world.' What do you think *parody* means?

a satire or spoof ______

b joke or yarn ______

c imitation or copy ______

d example or sample ______

3 Circle which of the following Terry does **not** enjoy.

a writing about evil characters

b sitting down and writing sixty-five thousand words

c receiving manuscripts from writers looking to get published

d chocolate

4 Tick (✓) the correct answer. In paragraph 1, why is the line 'Can we have more Death in this book?' humorous?

a Young people like reading stories where characters die. ______

b Death is a popular character. ______

c 'Death' is a pun—it has two meanings here. ______

d Death is Terry's favourite character. ______

5 Why are the interviewer's questions in **bold**? Underline two possible answers.

a to break up the small print

b to show the difference between question and answer

c to make the page look attractive

d because we are more interested in what the interviewer has to say

6 Summarise in your own words Terry's advice to young writers (section 7).

____

____

____

____

____

____

7 Tick (✓) the correct answer. Why is the word '*it's*' written in italics in Terry's last answer?

- **a** because Terry knows what *it's* is ______
- **b** to show that Terry is 58 years old ______
- **c** to show that Terry uses stress to emphasise the word as he speaks it ______
- **d** when Terry says *it's* he means *it is* ______

8 Tick (✓) the correct answer. In the phrase 'Can anyone tell me what *it's* all about?' what do you believe *it* is?

- **a** a good story ______
- **b** the interview ______
- **c** Terry's age ______
- **d** the meaning of life ______

9 In section 8, Terry talks about how he thinks characters are an important feature of a good book. Read his answer and then write what makes a book good in your opinion.

____

____

____

10 Tick (✓) the correct answer. How would you best describe the tone of this interview?

- **a** depressed and unhappy ______
- **b** chatty and informative ______
- **c** mysterious and secretive ______
- **d** gossipy and informal ______

11 Do Terry Pratchett's books sound like the kind of books you would like to read? Why/Why not?

____

____

____

____

____

____

12 What was the most interesting or important thing you found out about writers and writing from the interview?

____

____

____

____

____

____

____

Boost your reading skills

Understanding text organisation (structure)

It is always important to look over a text to get an idea of its **structure** and the **organisation** of ideas. Paying attention to how a text is organised will help you see the text as a whole, and not as separate isolated pieces of information.

An interview is a structured conversation between two people. Its purpose is to present interesting and entertaining information to its readers.

- The opening, middle and ending of an interview each contain different types of questions. It is necessary to begin or open the interview with some **general introductory questions** that may be used to introduce the interviewee (the person being interviewed) or the general topic of the interview.
- Questions in the middle of the interview will be **more specific** and allow for a greater depth of response. Sometimes an interviewer will ask more than one question on a single idea in the middle of the interview.
- Special questions are used towards the end of the interview in order to **conclude** or **finalise** the interview itself.

1 Look at the following questions from a variety of other interviews. Label each an *O*, *M* or *E*:

O for opening interview questions
M for middle-of-interview questions
E for end-of-interview questions.

a What was the first thing you remember writing? ______

b What advice would you have for anyone who is thinking of writing? ______

c You were in a band once—what's your favourite band now? ______

d And what happened to your band? ______

e For those who don't know, what is a narrative? ______

f Do you have any final recommendations? ______

g How did you discover your talent? ______

h Your books are a bit unusual, aren't they? Have you had any problems getting them published? ______

i What would be a question to ask our audience? ______

j How did you go from that to getting a recording contract? ______

Work on words

Idioms and idiomatic expressions

An **idiom** is an **informal expression**, **word** or **phrase** where the words together have a meaning that is different from the dictionary definitions of the individual words themselves. *Idiom* means 'one of a kind' and indicates that a phrase is being used with a special meaning that can be very different to the literal meaning. If someone says, 'When Mrs Smith saw the mud tracks on the floor, she hit the roof' they actually mean that Mrs Smith was extremely angry, and not that she actually hit the roof.

An idiom is an informal or colloquial manner of speaking that is natural to native speakers of a language. It is often a feature of spoken language. In the interview, Terry Pratchett uses informal idiomatic expressions when answering the interview questions. This is because the interview is casual, and as he would like to also put his young audience at ease, he uses idioms to avoid being too proper or adult. The interview questions also reflect this informal approach and it is a feature of the nature and style of the publication 'Rollercoaster'.

1 Look at the following examples from the interview. What do you think Terry is saying?

a 'If you get this right then the writing is a piece of cake.' Is Terry saying that writing will be easy or difficult?

____

b When talking about the types of characters his readers want him to create, Terry says, 'What you want are the screwed up characters.' What type of characters is he talking about?

____

c When talking about what makes a good writer, Terry says, 'There's no magical holy grail.' What do you think he is trying to say about being a good writer (even if you don't know what *holy grail* means)?

____

d When giving ideas on writing, Terry says, 'There is no mystical map or anything like that.' Terry isn't actually talking about a real map. What is he saying about learning to be a writer?

____

e Terry says '… but at some point you have to apply the bum to the seat and knock out about sixty-five thousand words,' What does *knock out* mean? Circle the best two answers.

i triumph
ii create
iii thump
iv produce
v punch

2 Match the following **idiomatic expressions** to their correct meaning by connecting them with a line.

a Although she went to court, she was only given a slap on the wrist.	there was no better
b Wow! This dress costs an arm and a leg.	a mild punishment
c She was tickled pink by the present.	it is extremely expensive
d We're all in the same boat.	not healthy
e That was hands down the best dinner I've eaten all year.	made very glad
f He's a bit of a loose cannon.	all of us are in the same position
g That show is driving me up the wall!	unpredictable
h I've been feeling under the weather.	making me very irritated

3 Now look at these **idioms** and see if you can work out the meaning on your own.

a We have a lot to do so let's roll up our sleeves and get to work.

____

____

b Grandpa turned 97 last week. He's no spring chicken any more.

____

____

c I can't go to the movies this week as I'm really strapped for cash.

____

____

d I have a secret that I would really like to get off my chest.

____

____

e I paid too much for those boots. I was really taken for a ride.

____

____

f My daughter is the apple of my eye.

____

____

g You really hit the nail on the head with that response.

____

____

Spotlight on language

The language of interviews

An interview's purpose is to present interesting and entertaining information to its readers. The kind of language you choose when conducting and writing up an interview will make your interview authentic (real) and fun to read.

As a student, it's important to think about the differences between spoken and written language. Written language is often formal and follows strict rules, like the kind of writing you do in paragraphs, essays and reports. Spoken language, on the other hand, is informal and written the way we 'speak'. An **interview** is often written using the features of **spoken language** as it is a **transcript** (record) of a real conversation.

Feature of spoken language	Examples
Fillers are words which do not carry conventional meaning but which are inserted in speech to allow time to think, to create a pause or to hold a turn in conversation.	*er, um, ah, OK, kinda*

1 Find two examples of fillers that Terry uses when speaking.

Feature of spoken language	Example
Pauses are breaks in speech that are used for a range of effects: thinking time, hesitation, waiting for a response or to indicate that a turn in the conversation is complete.	Pauses are often shown using ellipsis (…).

2 Write the example of a pause in Terry's thoughts from section 3.

Feature of spoken language	Example
Technical language is specific vocabulary related to a specific task or occupation.	Computing is an area that has a language specific to its field (e.g. *mouse, hardware, download*).

3 Find three examples of words that Terry Pratchett uses that are special to his occupation as a writer.

Feature of spoken language	Example
Stress is often shown by underlining, **bolding** or *italicising* to show that a word has been said in a particular way (probably louder and with more force than other words to make a point).	The angry Parent said, "I asked **you** to empty the bin *immediately*!"

4 Find the example in the text where the author has used italics to communicate that Terry has spoken a word with stress (more force). Why was this word stressed?

Feature of spoken language	Example
Informal language is language that is often used in spoken texts and reflects the casual and relaxed nature of spoken conversation.	colloquial expressions—'Fair go, mate.' contractions—'Didn't you get it?' second-person pronoun 'you'—'*You* can get it from there.' short, sometimes incomplete sentences

5 Find three examples of informal words or expressions that Terry Pratchett uses in his interview answers (e.g. *honest buck, I just did.*).

Extend your skills

Write another three questions to ask Terry. Then answer them as Terry might—try to use his **informal** and **conversational style** of answering questions, including some features of spoken language. You will need to make up ideas about what he might say.

Questions that open an interview are very different from questions that are used in the middle or end of an interview. Your question should be suitable for its location within the interview.

Question 1: beginning of interview

Terry's response:

Question 2: middle of interview

Terry's response:

Question 3: end of interview

Terry's response:

UNIT FIVE

Information text

Before you read

When you **predict**, you use information from pictures, words and personal experiences to **anticipate** what you will read. If you start thinking about what you are about to read before you read, it will make it easier to follow the meaning of the text as you read.

Look only at the images presented in the following newsletter—not the written information.

1 What do you think is the main topic/area/idea that these images are associated with?

____

____

2 Read the opening paragraph of the text below and quickly skim the other paragraphs. Write down as many key words or ideas from the text that you remember after one reading.

____

____

____

Wombat High newsletter

WOMBAT HIGH NEWSLETTER

October Issue no. 11

Student leadership issue

1 At Wombat High, we pride ourselves on the variety of leadership programs available to our students.

A Student Leader is a person of trust, a leader and mentor to other students. Becoming involved in student leadership at Wombat High is an opportunity for students to positively influence other students' experiences of study and school life. It is a chance to motivate new students to connect with friends, enjoy a rich experience and succeed in study.

Over the past few newsletters we have been focusing on the different **skills** necessary for strong leadership. In this issue, we will focus on what it means to be a **team leader**.

What is a team leader?

2 A **team leader** is someone who provides guidance, instruction, direction and leadership to a group of other students (the team) for the purpose of achieving a key result.

A **good team leader** listens constructively to their team and works with them to achieve goals that have been set.

3 The responsibilities of a team leader include team building and ensuring teamwork. The term 'team leader' is used to emphasise the cooperative nature of a team, in contrast to a typical command structure, where the head of a team would be its 'commander'.

4 Year 12 students have the most significant leadership responsibilities, including School Captains, House Captains and the Student Representative Council (SRC). All Student Representatives and Captains are expected to be representatives who exemplify school values. Their duties range from public speaking at school events to encouraging the involvement of other students.

5 Leadership involves:

- being able to motivate and direct others
- taking responsibility
- setting objectives
- organising and motivating others
- taking the initiative
- persevering when things are not working out
- accepting responsibility for mistakes/wrong decisions
- being flexible.

REMINDERS

PARENT TEACHER NIGHT – Tuesday 9th December

P&C Annual Meeting – Monday 15th December

Ph: 8971 7166 • Fax: 8777 6041

Email: info@wombathigh.nsw.edu.au • Website: www.wombathigh.nsw.edu.au

Test your understanding

1 Match each image below to their best title by connecting them with a line.

a 

b 

c 

team strategy | team leader | stand out from the crowd

2 Tick (✓) the correct answer. You may be familiar with the term *mentor*, but the word's meaning does change depending on the situation. Look at the word *mentor* in section 1 and choose the best synonym (similar word) for it.

a guide ______

b counsellor ______

c tutor ______

d instructor ______

3 Tick (✓) the correct answer. What is the overall purpose of section 4?

a outline the roles and responsibilities of student leaders ______

b focus on leadership requirements ______

c define team leadership ______

d provide information on leadership opportunities ______

4 Connect the ideas from the newsletter to their best definition by drawing a line.

a leader	the people who make up the group/team
b guidance	involving shared participation in working towards a common goal
c key result	a person who offers direction and assistance
d cooperative	a main/significant outcome
e team	assistance/supervision/leadership

5 Tick (✓) the correct answer. Section 2 tells you that, 'a good team leader listens constructively to their team'. The words *listen constructively* mean

a listen and then deliver an order. ______

b listen and then seek further advice. ______

c half-listen. ______

d listen in a useful and helpful way. ______

6 Read section 3. Using your own words, what do you think are the main differences between a *team leader* and a *team commander*?

____

____

____

7 Tick (✓) the correct answer. In the opening sentence, 'At Wombat High, we pride ourselves on the variety of leadership programs available to our students', what does *we pride ourselves* mean?

a We provide better leadership opportunities than all the other schools in the area. ______

b We are very proud of the variety of leadership opportunities at our school. ______

c We want all our students to have access to a variety of leadership opportunities. ______

d We are confident about our leaders. ______

8 Place each leadership term from section 5 in the correct sentence. The first one has been done for you.

motivate	initiative	objectives	persevering	responsibility	flexible

a Creating ___objectives___ as a team and sticking with them will help your team reach their goals.

b A team leader can really ______________ their team if they offer good guidance and instruction.

c It is the ______________ of the team leader to ensure that the teamwork cooperatively together.

d In ______________ through difficulties, it is possible to reach a positive outcome.

e Being ______________ is an important skill when working with a group as a team.

f Being a person who takes ______________ will offer guidance to those who work with you.

9 In your own words, why do you think Wombat High has decided to focus on 'team leaders' as an important leadership skill?

Boost your reading skills

Note-taking and paraphrasing

Paraphrasing is using your own words to express someone else's ideas without changing the original meaning.

Students often use paraphrasing when note-taking. These ideas may then be reused for an essay or assignment. Paraphrasing is a crucial skill that will allow you to use your own ideas when writing, rather than risking plagiarism (using others' ideas without referencing their work or changing the information).

1 Read through the following points and then fill in the **note-taking** scaffold below.

- Read the Wombat High newsletter carefully, and make sure that you understand exactly what the writer is saying. Highlight the main points as you read.
- Put the original aside and try to explain the main ideas in your own words.
- Check that you have kept the original meaning.
- Change words or phrases that match the original too closely.

Write the source (location) of your information here. You may need to find it again or create a bibliography. Be precise about the source details, for example title, dates and page numbers.

Main ideas: write the main ideas in your own words in the space. The first one has been done for you.

Student leader:

A student leader counsels and guides other students in a relationship that relies on trust. Student leadership experiences enrich a student's academic and social life and lead to success.

Team leader:

Leadership involves:

Features of a good team leader:

Comments: write down any questions that occur to you from the reading. You may like to write down a list of words that you did not know and that require checking in a dictionary.

Work on words

Synonyms

A **synonym** is a word that **means** the **same** (or nearly the same) as another word, such as *strong* and *robust*. Synonyms can be useful when summarising other people's ideas in your own words. Actively thinking about and working on synonyms will increase your vocabulary and ability to describe.

When talking about synonyms we can use the following phrases:

- … is another word for …
- … means the same thing as …
- … is a synonym for …

1 Using the word bank, fill in the sentences below.

common	malicious	hesitant	vulnerable	contentment

a ______________ is another word for *happiness*.

b *Spiteful* means the same thing as ______________.

c ______________ is a synonym for *helplessness*.

d *Popular* is another word for ______________.

e ______________ means the same thing as *unsure*.

An **antonym** is a word that means the **opposite** of another word.

For example: The word *wet* is an antonym, or opposite, of the word *dry*.

2 Place either *S* for **synonym** or *A* for **antonym** next to the following groups of words. The first one has been done for you.

a agree, disagree ___A___

b cold, freezing ______

c fragment, piece ______

d argue, squabble ______

e guess, estimate ______

f bottom, highest ______

g tired, energetic ______

h ruin, destroy ______

i descend, float ______

j gusty, tranquil ______

k raucous, silent ______

l persuade, convince ______

3 The following sentences are from the newsletter. Find a **synonym** for the underlined words in each sentence. You may like to use a dictionary or a thesaurus.

A thesaurus is a very helpful reference book that lists words in groups of synonyms.

a A team <u>leader</u> is someone who provides <u>guidance</u>, instruction and direction and leadership to a group of other students.

____

____

____

b A <u>good</u> team leader listens constructively to their team and works with them to <u>achieve</u> goals that have been set.

____

____

____

____

c A Student Leader is a person of trust, a leader and mentor to other students.

____

d Becoming involved in student leadership at Wombat High is an opportunity for students to positively influence other students' experiences of study and school life.

____

____

e It is a chance to motivate new students to connect with friends, enjoy a rich experience and succeed in study.

____

____

4 Section 5 from the newsletter contains a number of important leadership terms. For each example from section 5, underline the best two **synonyms** that show its meaning. The first one has been done for you.

a	Motivate:	encourage	examine	inspire	produce	investigate
b	Initiative:	skill	ingenuity	obligation	resourcefulness	inactivity
c	Objective:	goal	creation	disagreement	aim	task
d	Persevering:	determined	kind	motivating	purposeful	inflexible
e	Responsibility:	consideration	accountability	promptness	duty	freedom
f	Flexible:	bendable	rigid	in control	creative	malleable

Spotlight on language

Neutral language

The Wombat High newsletter uses language which avoids expressing a personal opinion or attitude towards the topic. Instead it keeps the language **neutral**. Neutral language helps make the information appear **reliable**, **factual** and **objective**.

For example:
The responsibilities of a team leader include team building and ensuring teamwork.

This is an example of language that is neutral. It does not contain emotive language, which may manipulate, influence or create feelings in the reader.

Neutral language is one aspect of **formal language**—that is, the kind of language we mostly use in factual texts.

When writing formally you should:

- avoid personal pronouns (e.g. *I*, *you* or *we*)
- avoid verbs that show emotion and feeling (e.g. *I think* or *I am pleased*)
- use words that are particular to the topic being discussed. (These are called 'technical words'. See Unit 10 for more on technical words.)

1 Read the following sentences. Out of each pair, underline the example which gives the information in a neutral, **objective** way, and is not emotional or exaggerated. The first one has been done for you.

- **a** <u>The news program was significant and provided background information.</u>

  The news program was fascinating and provided background information.
- **b** The politician was snobbish and voters could not stand him.

  The politician was reserved and unpopular with his voters.
- **c** The newsreader had a cheery way of speaking.

  The newsreader had an engaging way of speaking.
- **d** The behaviour of the students was not at all impressive.

  The behaviour of the students was really disgusting.
- **e** The new team leader was fussy about details.

  The new team leader was meticulous and thorough.

2 Remove the **personal pronouns** and **emotive language** from these sentences and rewrite them.

- **a** I believe a cool team leader is a person like you who provides guidance, instruction, direction and leadership to a group of other individuals.

  ____

  ____

  ____

  ____

- **b** We don't think the team members should directly report or answer to the team leader but we think they should be expected to provide support to the team leader in achieving the group's brilliant goals.

  ____

  ____

  ____

  ____

  ____

3 Underline the words that are particular to the topic (leadership). The first one has been done for you.

- **a** A <u>team leader</u> is someone who provides guidance, instruction, direction and <u>leadership</u> to a group of other students (<u>the team</u>) for the purpose of achieving a <u>key result</u>.
- **b** A good team leader listens constructively to their team and works with them to achieve goals that have been set.
- **c** The term *team leader* is used to emphasise the cooperative nature of a team, in contrast to a typical command structure where the head of a team would be its *commander*.

Extend your skills

Using the note-taking scaffold below, find another text to read and summarise. You may like to choose a chapter from a school textbook that you need to study from, or a website that you are using for an upcoming essay or assignment. The more you practise **summarising** and **note-taking**, the easier it will become. Don't forget that using synonyms for key words can help you put others' ideas into your own words.

Source:

Main ideas:

Comments:

UNIT SIX

Reading Shakespeare

Before you read

It is important to be an active reader. Part of this is to keep **thinking about** and **predicting** what is to come in the text. This helps you understand the **main theme** and **overall focus** of the text.

Read only the first two paragraphs below, extracted from the *Tales from Shakespeare*.

1 Based on the information given about the two families in paragraph one, what do you think *enmity* (line 3) means?

____

____

____

2 Tick (✓) the correct answer. What do you think the purpose of the remaining two paragraphs will be?

a continue to focus on the feuding families ______

b provide more detailed information about the great supper (party) ______

c introduce more characters ______

Tales from Shakespeare—*Romeo and Juliet*

1 The two chief families in Verona were the rich Capulets and the Montagues. There had been an old quarrel between these families, which had grown to a great height, and so deadly was the enmity between them, that it extended to the remotest kindred and to the followers and retainers of both sides. So much so that a servant of the house of Montague could not meet a servant of the house of Capulet, nor a Capulet encounter with a Montague by chance, but fierce words and sometimes bloodshed ensued. Frequent were the brawls from such accidental meetings, which disturbed the happy quiet of Verona's streets.

2 Old Lord Capulet made a great supper, to which many fair ladies and many noble guests were invited. All the admired beauties of Verona were present, and all comers were made welcome if they were not of the house of Montague. At this feast of Capulets, Rosaline, beloved of Romeo, son to the old Lord Montague, was present; and though it was dangerous for a Montague to be seen in this assembly, yet Benvolio, a friend of Romeo, persuaded the young lord to go to this assembly in the disguise of a mask, that he might see his Rosaline, and, seeing her, compare her with some choice beauties of Verona, who (he said) would make him think his swan a crow.

3 Romeo had small faith in Benvolio's words; nevertheless, for the love of Rosaline, he was persuaded to go. For Romeo was a sincere and passionate lover, and one that lost his sleep for love and fled society to be alone, thinking on Rosaline, who disdained him and never requited his love with the least show of courtesy or affection; and Benvolio wished to cure his friend of this love by showing him diversity of ladies and company.

4 To this feast of Capulets, then, young Romeo, with Benvolio and their friend Mercutio, went masked. Old Capulet bid them welcome and told them that ladies who had their toes unplagued with corns would dance with them.

And the old man was light-hearted and merry, and said that he had worn a mask when he was young and could have told a whispering tale in a fair lady's ear. And they fell to dancing, and Romeo was suddenly struck with the exceeding beauty of a lady who danced there, who seemed to him to teach the torches to burn bright, and her beauty to show by night like a rich jewel worn by a blackamoor; beauty too rich for use, too dear for earth! Like a snowy dove trooping with crows (he said), so richly did her beauty and perfections shine above the ladies her companions.

Source: http://www.world-english.org/stories_romeo_juliet.htm

Test your understanding

1 Match the character names to their best description.

Capulets and Montagues	Romeo's close friend
Romeo	a girl with whom Romeo is infatuated, but who does not return his love
Benvolio	the head and leader of the Capulet family
Rosaline	son of the old Lord Montague
Old Lord Capulet	wealthy feuding families of Verona

2 In which order do these events occur? Number them from 1 to 5.

a ______ When dancing, Romeo's eye is caught by a beautiful young girl who is not Rosaline.

b ______ Romeo and Benvolio are welcomed to the party by Lord Capulet.

c ______ The head of the Capulet family is organising a grand party.

d ______ The reader learns of the hostility between the Montague and Capulet families.

e ______ Benvolio persuades Romeo to attend the party using a mask as a disguise.

3 Tick (✓) the correct answer. What was Benvolio's purpose in encouraging Romeo to attend the party?

a Benvolio wanted to encourage Romeo's romance with Rosaline. ______

b Benvolio wanted to upset the party with the presence of Montagues. ______

c Benvolio wanted Romeo to view other young ladies so that he might forget Rosaline. ______

d Benvolio thought the party may cure Romeo of an illness. ______

4 Tick (✓) the correct answer. At the end of paragraph 2, Benvolio says that Romeo 'might see his Rosaline, and, seeing her compare her with some choice beauties of Verona, who (he said) would make him think his swan a crow'. Why do you think the author uses parentheses, also known as brackets, *(he said)*, in this sentence?

a to show that Romeo does not necessarily agree with Benvolio ______

b to show that Benvolio is the speaker ______

c to show that Benvolio is correct ______

d to show that Romeo thinks like Benvolio ______

5 In paragraph 4, we learn that Old Montague, when he was young, 'could have told a whispering tale in a fair lady's ear'. Using your own words, describe what you think this reveals about his character.

6 Think about what you have read so far. What is your opinion of each of the following? Circle your answer and give a reason for your choice.

a the character of Romeo: sincere playful senseless

b Benvolio: risk-taker genuine troublemaker

c the feud between the families: pointless honourable necessary

Boost your reading skills

Deducing the meaning of words

When reading, you often have to **deduce**, or work out, the meanings of words you have not seen before. This may involve using a dictionary to locate an exact definition or using clues, as well as your background knowledge, to 'guess' what the word may mean.

1 Circle the word(s) that you think is closest in **meaning** to the word in italics, using the underlined information to help you. The first one has been done for you.

a The feud between the families extended to the remotest *kindred,* to the followers and retainers of both sides. (lines 6–7)

kindred: family enemies admirers

b Benvolio wished to cure his friend of this love by showing him *diversity* of ladies and company. (lines 37–39)

diversity: similar variety group

c Romeo was suddenly *struck* with the exceeding beauty of a lady who danced there

struck: discovered collided with affected by

d … so richly did her beauty and perfections *shine* above the ladies her companions.

shine: polish radiate appear

e Frequent were the brawls from such accidental meetings, which *disturbed* the happy quiet of Verona's streets.

disturbed: interrupted woke up disappointed

Prefixes 'un' and 'dis'

Knowing about **prefixes** is useful in understanding and spelling words. A prefix is a group of letters at the beginning of a word that partly shows its meaning. Two common prefixes are *un* and *dis*, both meaning 'not' or 'the opposite of'.

For example: *un* + likely → unlikely *un* + professional → unprofessional
dis + comfort → discomfort *dis* + order → disorder

2 Use your knowledge of the **prefixes** *un* and *dis* to help you understand and then write the meanings of the italicised words.

a Benvolio, a friend of Romeo, persuaded the young lord to go to this assembly in the *disguise* of a mask (lines 24–26)

guise: appearance/facade

disguise: ______________________

b Old Capulet bid them welcome and told them that ladies who had their toes *unplagued* with corns would dance with them (lines 42–44)

plagued: afflicted/diseased

unplagued: ______________________

c They were *dispossessed* of land and properties.

possessed: owned

dispossessed: ______________________

d The meeting was *unofficial* and took the employees by surprise.

official: authorised/approved

unofficial: ______________________

e The storm was *unforseen* and completely ruined their holiday plans.

foreseen: expected/anticipated

unforeseen: ______________________

f The twins, despite appearing identical, were *dissimilar* in all other ways.

similar: comparable/alike

dissimilar: ______________________________

Work on words

Shakespeare's language

Although this is a simplified and modern excerpt of Shakespeare's original story, it still retains some **formality** and sense of Shakespeare's original style and language.

Language during the Elizabethan period was more formal than it is now. Shakespeare used this formality in language to make phrases sound more **poetic**, as well as to help him create **rhythm**.

1 Look at the following examples of language from the excerpt. Write the **modern equivalent** to the underlined words in the space provided. The first one has been done for you.

a There had been an old quarrel between these families, which had grown to a great height (line 2) increased, worsened, intensified

b ... but fierce words and sometimes bloodshed ensued (line 11)

____

c ... and all comers were made welcome if they were not of the house of Montague (line 18)

____

d ... thinking on Rosaline who disdained him and never requited his love (lines 35–36)

____

e And they fell to dancing (lines 48–49)

____

2 Find a word in the text that **means**

a 'foremost' (line 1) ______________________________

b 'scuffle' (line 12) ______________________________

c 'attractive' (line 6) ______________________________

d 'politeness' (line 37) ______________________________

Spotlight on language

Imagery—similes and metaphors

Imagery allows writers to use words and language to 'paint a picture' in their readers' minds. It can add depth and understanding to what you are reading and may help you further appreciate writers' ideas. There are two main kinds of imagery in the *Romeo and Juliet* excerpt—similes and metaphors.

A **simile** is an expression that **directly compares two different things**, usually by using the words *like* or *as*.

For example:

He fights **like** a lion. (He is strong.)

The road was **as** straight **as** an arrow. (The road has no bends.)

A **metaphor** is a type of image where **something is said to be something else**. Unlike similes, you don't use *like* or *as* in the comparison.

For example:

The cheetah **was** a lightning bolt and caught its prey. (The cheetah was very fast.)

Love **is** a rose. (Love is beautiful.)

Look at the following underlined examples from the excerpt. Mark each one either *M* for **metaphor** or *S* for **simile**, and then answer the questions.

1 **a** '… beauty too rich for use, too dear for earth! Like a snowy dove trooping with crows, so richly did her beauty and perfections shine above the ladies her companions.' ______

b Who is like a snowy dove? ______

c Who are the crows? ______

d What image (picture) of Juliet is placed in the readers' minds?

______

______

______

2 **a** 'Romeo was suddenly struck with the exceeding beauty of a lady who danced there … and her beauty to show by night like a rich jewel worn by a blackamoor' (Note: a *blackamoor* was a term used by Elizabethans to describe a dark-skinned person, usually from Africa.) ______

b What is like a rich jewel? ______

c What image (picture) of Juliet is placed in the readers' minds?

______

______

______

3 **a** 'Benvolio, a friend of Romeo, persuaded the young lord to go to this assembly in the disguise of a mask, that he might see his Rosaline, and, seeing her, compare her with some choice beauties of Verona, who (he said) would make him think his swan a crow'. ______

b Who thinks Rosaline is a swan? ____________________

c Is this a positive or negative image?

d Explain your reason.

e Who thinks Roasaline is a crow?

f Is this a positive or negative image?

g Explain your reason.

Extend your skills

The story is continued for you below; however, the paragraphs are placed out of order. Number them in the correct order. The first one has been done for you.

1

a __1__ While he uttered these praises he was overheard by Tybalt, a nephew of Lord Capulet, who knew him by his voice to be Romeo.

b ______ It being midnight, Romeo with his companions departed; but they soon missed him, for, unable to stay away from the house where he had left his heart, he leaped the wall of an orchard which was at the back of Juliet's house.

c ______ But his uncle, the old Lord Capulet, would not suffer him to do any injury at that time, both out of respect to his guests and because Romeo had borne himself like a gentleman and all tongues in Verona bragged of him to be a virtuous and well-governed youth.

d ______ Tybalt, forced to be patient against his will, restrained himself, but swore that this vile Montague should at another time dearly pay for his intrusion.

e ______ And this Tybalt, being of a fiery and passionate temper, could not endure that a Montague should come under cover of a mask, to fleer and scorn (as he said) at their solemnities. And he stormed and raged exceedingly, and would have struck young Romeo dead.

f ______ Here he had not been long, ruminating on his new love, when Juliet appeared above at a window, through which her exceeding beauty seemed to break like the light of the sun in the east; and the moon, which shone in the orchard with a faint light, appeared to Romeo as if sick and pale with grief at the superior lustre of this new sun.

UNIT SEVEN

Picture book

Before you read

When you read, you often make **connections** to other texts you have read and seen and to experiences from your own life. Making these connections will help you understand and **decode** (make sense of) new texts.

1 What do you know about the nature and personality of possums?

Possums are generally: ____________________

2 What do you know about the nature and personality of rabbits?

Rabbits are generally: ____________________

3 What are your first impressions of the picture book page below?

____

'The Building of the Houses' from *The Rabbits*

Image reproduced with permission from The Rabbits by John Marsden and Shaun Tan, Lothian Children's Books, an imprint of Hachette Australia, 1998.

Background to the text: This picture book is told from the viewpoint of native animals that look like possums. The book examines the consequences of the arrival of a group of rabbits who have an entirely unfamiliar way of life. They bring new food and animals, and they make their own houses to live in, eventually dominating the environment and its native inhabitants.

Test your understanding

Tick (✓) the best answer for each of the following questions.

1 Look at the image from the book and read the words around the images. Who does the word *they* in the text refer to?

- **a** the rabbits ______
- **b** the possums ______
- **c** buildings ______
- **d** trees ______

2 Who does the word *we* in the text refer to?

- **a** rabbits ______
- **b** clouds ______
- **c** possums ______
- **d** paintings ______

3 Look at the background information written above. In the final line '… eventually dominating the environment and its native inhabitants', who is dominating the environment and its native inhabitants?

- **a** the possums ______
- **b** the large tree ______
- **c** the rabbits ______
- **d** the large painting ______

4 Which word could replace the word *dominating* in '… eventually dominating the environment and its native inhabitants'?

- **a** helping ______
- **b** taking over ______
- **c** resisting ______
- **d** damaging ______

5 The story is told from which of the animals' perspective (point of view)?

____

Which words or images give you this idea?

____

____

____

6 Look at the animals depicted to the right and left of the large painting. They are rabbits. Did you realise this?

If not, what did you think they were?

7 In what ways do the rabbits in the picture book image appear similar to normal rabbits?

8 In what ways do the rabbits in the picture book image appear different from normal rabbits?

9 Using the following Venn diagram, write words to describe the rabbits' and possums' differences in the outer circles, and show their similarities or things they have in common in the centre circle. Some words have been added to help you.

possums
natural
in the trees
both are animals
stern
rabbits
wearing clothes

10 Tick (✓) the best answer. The rabbits are holding a picture. Look at it closely and think about the wording on the page. What do you think the picture shows?

a the place the rabbits have come from ______
b the possums' new homes ______
c the rabbits' new homes ______
d the rabbits' favourite place ______

11 Do you like the rabbits or the possums the best?

What influenced your decision?

12 Tick (✓) the best answer. Who is the intended audience for this picture book?

a children ______
b teenagers ______
c adults ______
d children and adults ______

13 What influenced your decision? Look at the images and the language to help you answer this question.

____

____

____

____

14 Does the author want us to feel sorry for the rabbits or the possums?

____

Why do you think this?

____

____

____

15 Tick (✓) the answer you think is correct. This picture book has been interpreted in a few ways. Some people think the book has a deeper meaning, and that the rabbits and possums might actually symbolise (stand for) something else.

a The rabbits represent teachers and the possums represent students. ______

b The rabbits represent politicians and the possums represent everyday Australians. ______

c The rabbits represent white colonisers and the possums represent Indigenous Australians. ______

d The rabbits represent business people and the possums represent the self-employed. ______

Boost your reading skills

Reading visual texts

The language mode of **viewing** refers to analysing any text that contains graphic or visual elements such as pictures, graphs, illustrations or even moving images. Such texts are called **multimedia** texts. Multimedia texts may use words to communicate ideas as well. Newspaper articles, for example, often contain photographs, charts and illustrations that are essential to understanding the meaning of the article. Most web pages are also multimedia in content. They contain a visual component that includes font, headlines, pictures, diagrams and even moving images which must be analysed for full understanding.

Examples of multimedia texts that include visual features include:

- TV/print advertisements
- movies
- picture books
- comics
- brochures
- websites
- book covers

- posters
- art
- postcards
- photographs
- picture books
- book covers.

Visual literacy is the ability to understand and interpret information presented in the form of an image. Visual literacy is based on the ideas that pictures can be 'read'. Taking note of the **position** of items within an image and the **body language** of characters, as well as what **clothing** characters are wearing, can help you analyse an image for meaning.

Position means the location of objects, shapes and figures in the picture. Objects in the centre and foreground (front) are usually the point of interest and importance.

1 Match the different elements from *The Rabbits* to their position within the text by joining them with a line.

a top of the page	the painting
b foreground (centre front)	the collapsing buildings
c mid-ground (middle)	two rabbits
d featured in the background	the possums

2 Tick (✓) the best answer. Why has the illustrator chosen to place the painting in a position of importance and interest?

a The rabbits are presenting the possums with a gift. ______

b The painting represents/symbolises the rabbits' plan/vision for their future. ______

c The painting shows where the rabbits have come from. ______

d The rabbits highly value art and paintings. ______

Body language can communicate how figures are feeling and convey information about their personalities. For both the possums and the rabbits, circle the best four words that describe their body language.

3 How do the possums look?

curious bored natural conversational excited watchful rigid

4 How do the rabbits look?

stiff fun-loving purposeful angry upright helpful ordered

Clothing can also give very significant clues about character and personality.

5 **a** Describe the rabbits' clothing/attire.

____

____

b The possums are wearing nothing. Why do you think the illustrator has clothed the rabbits but not the possums?

____

____

c Who looks more powerful?

____

Why do you think this?

____

____

Work on words

Interpreting symbols

Human beings communicate through the use of **symbols**. Symbols are things that stand for or represent something else. They may be visual or aural (sound). When we interpret symbols in visual images we do so using specific knowledge, just as we do when reading written language.

Our world is filled with visual symbols that we recognise and respond to daily. These symbols represent everyday necessities and information that we rely on.

1 Label these common **symbols** according to what they usually mean in everyday life.

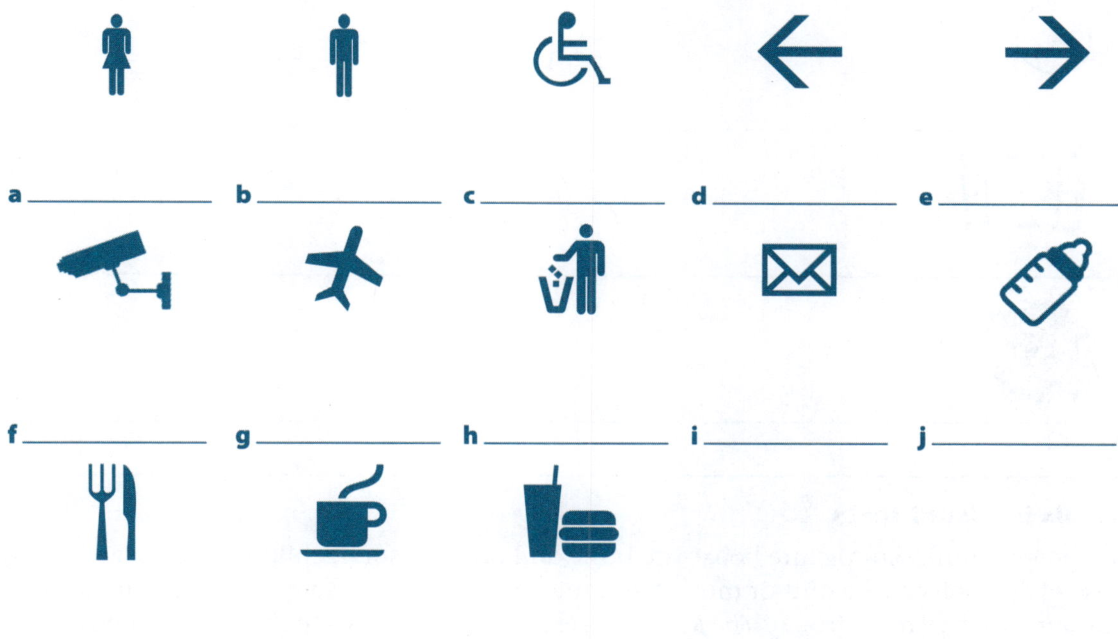

a ____________ b ____________ c ____________ d ____________ e ____________

f ____________ g ____________ h ____________ i ____________ j ____________

k ____________ l ____________ m ____________

Many symbols have **connotations**—that is, **meanings** and **interpretations** beyond the meaning of the symbol itself.

For example, if we see a man giving a woman a red rose we might assume or conclude that the man is in love with the woman. In this case, we have looked beyond our basic understanding of a rose and drawn a deeper conclusion—a red rose symbolises love.

2 Look at the following images and describe what they may further **symbolise** or **represent**. The first one has been done for you.

Symbol	Possible meaning(s)
	love, romance, relationships, valentine, femininity

Symbols in visual texts

Many people think that picture books are basic and only for small children; however, through the use of symbolism, the author may communicate deeper and more sophisticated messages about our society. This is true of *The Rabbits*. The main characters—the rabbits and possums—are actually symbols for other ideas.

In this way, the text acts as an **allegory**—a text with two meanings that has a **literal** meaning and a **symbolic** meaning. An allegory is a story, poem or picture that can be interpreted to reveal a hidden meaning, typically a moral or political one.

The Rabbits explores present-day feelings, struggles and tensions that are in Australia about Indigenous rights, the stolen generation, colonisation and reconciliation. It shows aspects of Australia's colonisation by the British from the point of view of the Indigenous population, the Aborigines.

3 Fill in the following table, focusing on **symbolism** and what the symbolism implies in *The Rabbits*. Some of the answers have been done for you.

Item/character	What they symbolise	What the symbol further suggests
possums		natural, unprotected, innocent
rabbits	invaders, colonisers	
rabbits' clothes		military, war, aggression, hostility, conflict, threat
wheel	technology	
clock		order, calendar, deadlines, business
tree	nature	
eyeglass		education, advancement, knowledge, information, scrutiny, inspection, examination

Spotlight on language

Reading paths

There is a special language used when discussing visual language features.

The **reading path** is the path, or direction, our eyes take when we view and process a visual image. The reading path begins with the **salient** elements of the image. A salient element or object is the feature of a visual image that stands out and grabs our attention the most. The path begins with the most salient object and then moves on to other less salient features.

1 Looking at the picture book page, circle which object you think is the **salient object**.

the rabbits | the trees | the buildings | the painting | the clouds

2 After choosing the **salient object**, write down the next three things your eyes notice when viewing the picture book page.

a ______________________

b ______________________

c ______________________

3 Did you notice the possums last?

____

This may be because they are located in the upper area of the page, and not in a noticeable position. Why do you think the illustrator placed them here?

____

____

____

Vectors are lines that lead the reader from one element to another. The lines may be visible or invisible. The lines may be created by characters within the image—through gaze, pointed fingers or extended arms.

A **horizontal vector** exists at the top of the picture book page. It is just below where the possums are sitting in their tree.

4 The illustrator has used the **horizontal vector** here as a divider. What do you think is being divided?

____

____

____

The **direction** that figures face is significant—the **gaze** (where they are looking), as well as **social distance** (distance between figures and characters) can communicate information about personalities and relationships.

5 **a** What **direction**(s) are the rabbits facing?

____

b Are they looking at the possums? ________________________

c Are the rabbits close to the possums? ________________________

d What do the rabbits' gazes reveal about their personalities?

____

____

6 **a** What **direction**(s) are the possums facing?

____

b Are they looking at the rabbits? ________________________

c Why are the possums in the tree?

____

____

d What does the **social distance** between the rabbits and the possums reveal about their relationship?

____

____

Extend your skills

The page from *The Rabbits* that you have just looked at occurs near the beginning of the original picture book. The next page's words read:

> They brought new food, and they brought other animals. We liked some of the food and we liked some of the animals. But some of the food made us sick, and some of the animals scared us.

1 Use your own words to describe the images and pictures you think would accompany the above words in the picture book *The Rabbits*.

2 What words do you think might appear on the page that follows this one? Try to follow the style of the book's words and use *they*, *we* and *us*.

UNIT EIGHT

Novel extract

Before you read

Reading a text is always easier if we know a little about **what to expect**. *Alice's Adventures in Wonderland* by Lewis Carroll was written in 1865 and is considered a children's classic that is still very popular today among people young and old.

Write down any words, knowledge or expectations you have of this story on the lines provided. Even if you have not read the story, you may know something of the book's characters, settings or events, or you may have even seen one of the *Alice in Wonderland* films.

___

___

___

Alice's Adventures in Wonderland by Lewis Carroll

Down the Rabbit Hole

1 Alice was beginning to get very tired of sitting by her sister on the bank, and of having nothing to do: once or twice she had peeped into the book her sister was reading, but it had no pictures or conversations in it, 'and what is the use of a book,' thought Alice 'without pictures or conversation?'

2 So she was considering in her own mind (as well as she could, for the hot day made her feel very sleepy and stupid), whether the pleasure of making a daisy-chain would be worth the trouble of getting up and picking the daisies, when suddenly a White Rabbit with pink eyes ran close by her.

3 There was nothing so very remarkable in that; nor did Alice think it so very much out of the way to hear the Rabbit say to itself, 'Oh dear! Oh dear! I shall be late!' (when she thought it over afterwards, it occurred to her that she ought to have wondered at this, but at the time it all seemed quite natural); but when the Rabbit actually took a watch out of its waistcoat pocket, and looked at it, and then hurried on, Alice started to her feet, for it flashed across her mind that she had never before seen a rabbit with either a waistcoat-pocket, or a watch to take out of it, and burning with curiosity, she ran across the field after it, and fortunately was just in time to see it pop down a large rabbit-hole under the hedge.

4 In another moment down went Alice after it, never once considering how in the world she was to get out again.

5 The rabbit-hole went straight on like a tunnel for some way, and then dipped suddenly down, so suddenly that Alice had not a moment to think about stopping herself before she found herself falling down a very deep well.

6 Either the well was very deep, or she fell very slowly, for she had plenty of time as she went down to look about her and to wonder what was going to happen next. First, she tried to look down and make out what she was coming to, but it was too dark to see anything; then she looked at the sides of the well, and noticed that they were filled with cupboards and book-shelves; here and there she saw maps and pictures hung upon pegs. She took down a jar from one of the shelves as she passed; it was labelled 'ORANGE MARMALADE', but to her

great disappointment it was empty: she did not like to drop the jar for fear of killing somebody, so managed to put it into one of the cupboards as she fell past it.

7 'Well!' thought Alice to herself, 'after such a fall as this, I shall think nothing of tumbling down stairs! How brave they'll all think me at home! Why, I wouldn't say anything about it, even if I fell off the top of the house!' (Which was very likely true.)

8 Down, down, down. Would the fall *NEVER* come to an end! 'I wonder how many miles I've fallen by this time?' she said aloud. 'I must be getting somewhere near the centre of the earth. Let me see: that would be four thousand miles down, I think—' (for, you see, Alice had learnt several things of this sort in her lessons in the schoolroom, and though this was not a *VERY* good opportunity for showing off her knowledge, as there was no one to listen to her, still it was good practice to say it over) '—yes, that's about the right distance—but then I wonder what Latitude or Longitude I've got to?' (Alice had no idea what Latitude was, or Longitude either, but thought they were nice grand words to say.)

9 Presently she began again. 'I wonder if I shall fall right *THROUGH* the earth! How funny it'll seem to come out among the people that walk with their heads downward! The Antipathies, I think—' (she was rather glad there was no one listening, this time, as it didn't sound at all the right word) '—but I shall have to ask them what the name of the country is, you know. Please, Ma'am, is this New Zealand or Australia?' (and she tried to curtsey as she spoke—fancy *CURTSEYING* as you're falling through the air! Do you think you could manage it?) 'And what an ignorant little girl she'll think me for asking! No, it'll never do to ask: perhaps I shall see it written up somewhere.'

Source: http://www.gutenberg.org/ebooks/928

Test your understanding

1 Tick (✓) the correct answer. At what point in the story do you think this extract is taken from?

a beginning ______

b middle ______

c end ______

2 Provide a reason for your answer to Question 1.

____

____

____

3 In which order do these events occur? Number them 1 to 5.

a ______ The White Rabbit runs past Alice, surprising her.

b ______ Alice grabs a jar labelled 'ORANGE MARMALADE'.

c ______ Alice gets tired of sitting next to her sister on the bank.

d ______ Alice wonders if she's in Australia.

e ______ Alice drops down the rabbit hole after the White Rabbit.

4 Why do you think Alice believes there is no value in a book 'without pictures or conversation'?

____

____

____

5 Tick (✓) the correct answer. What was Alice considering in her mind when the White Rabbit ran past her?

- **a** whether she could find the energy to collect some flowers and make a chain ______
- **b** peeping at her sister's book ______
- **c** how much she liked orange marmalade ______
- **d** finding a book with pictures and conversations ______

6 Tick (✓) the correct answer. Why did it occur to Alice that she should have questioned the White Rabbit saying, 'Oh dear! Oh dear! I shall be late!'?

- **a** She wondered why the rabbit was so late. ______
- **b** It is very unusual and unexpected to see a rabbit talking. ______
- **c** Alice has often seen rabbits walking and talking. ______
- **d** Alice expected the rabbit to say something entirely different. ______

7 In paragraph 4, after seeing the White Rabbit drop down the hole, we learn that '... down went Alice after it, never once considering how in the world she was to get out again'. What does this show about her personality and the type of person she is?

____

____

8 Tick (✓) the correct answer. Why, in paragraph 8, are the words *NEVER* and *VERY* written in capital letters?

- **a** Alice is shouting these words. ______
- **b** Alice is having trouble speaking as she is falling. ______
- **c** Alice is highlighting and reinforcing her ideas. ______
- **d** Alice is understating (lessening the importance of) her thoughts. ______

9 Tick (✓) the correct answer. In the line 'Alice had no idea what Latitude was, or Longitude either, but thought they were nice grand words to say', which word could replace *grand*?

- **a** inspiring ______
- **b** exciting ______
- **c** rousing ______
- **d** impressive ______

10 Tick (✓) the correct answer. Why does Alice believe she may be in New Zealand or Australia?

- **a** Alice has always wanted to travel to these places. ______
- **b** People in these countries enjoy eating orange marmalade. ______
- **c** Alice has learnt about these places at school. ______
- **d** Alice has been falling for so long she wonders if she has dropped through to the other side of the world. ______

11 Tick (✓) the correct answer. In paragraph 9 Alice, who is in England, mistakenly refers to New Zealand and Australia as the 'Antipathies'. What word do you think she actually means?

- **a** antonym—a word that means the opposite of another word ______
- **b** antipodes—any two places or regions that are on diametrically opposite sides of the earth. ______

c antiroyalist—someone opposed to the royal family ______

d antibodies—proteins generally found in the blood that detect and destroy invaders ______

12 Tick (✓) the correct answer. In paragraph 9 when Alice says, 'And what an ignorant little girl *she'll* think me for asking!' who is *she*?

a Alice's sister ______

b the Queen ______

c a woman in Australia or New Zealand ______

d the White Rabbit ______

13 What are your impressions of/feelings about Alice after reading this extract?

____

____

____

____

____

____

____

Boost your reading skills

Understanding complex sentences

In *Alice's Adventures in Wonderland,* the author has used many complex sentences. Readers get more information from complex sentences, and including them makes the story very descriptive, vivid and entertaining. When reading, don't skip over sentences because they look complicated and overwhelming—take note of where punctuation occurs (commas, dashes and semicolons) as these can help you slow down in order to 'digest' ideas. Identifying the main clause is also helpful and assists you to process important information.

There are three types of sentences in English: simple, compound and complex sentences. **Complex sentences** are made up of two clauses—an **independent** clause and a **dependent** clause. **Independent clauses** are similar to simple sentences. They can stand alone and function as a complete sentence.

For example: We didn't enter the building.
Harry won the competition.
My aunt will go ahead with her overseas holiday.

Dependent clauses are not complete sentences and are missing something in order for them to make sense. They need to be used together with an independent clause to make sense.

For example: despite it being open
because he had practiced for weeks
if she saves enough money

1 Review your knowledge of complex sentences. In the following sentences, underline the **independent** clause(s) and circle the **dependant** clause. The first one has been done for you.

- **a** Alexander has been working extremely hard (as there is an important assessment next week.)
- **b** If I leave for work at 8 am, I can usually walk to the beach early in the morning.
- **c** Although it was extremely expensive, Clarice bought the bag anyway.
- **d** Whenever Harry goes to the cinema, he enjoys going with his friend Paul.
- **e** I prefer to watch TV over the Internet as it allows me to watch what I want when I want.
- **f** If it looks like we are going to have heavy rain, I have to bring in the washing straight away.

2 Now look at these examples from *Alice's Adventures in Wonderland.* Underline the **independent** clause(s) and circle the **dependent** clause.

- **a** 'Alice started to her feet, for it flashed across her mind that she had never before seen a rabbit with either a waistcoat-pocket, or a watch to take out of it …'
- **b** 'In another moment down went Alice after it, never once considering how in the world she was to get out again.'
- **c** 'Why, I wouldn't say anything about it, even if I fell off the top of the house!'

Another good strategy to help follow complex sentences is to **break the text up** into smaller chunks of meaning. The *Alice's Adventures in Wonderland* extract contains many examples of long sentences that can appear hard to read and complicated. Look at the following example from the story. A slash (/) has been placed between each main idea in every sentence. In doing this, the sentence has been broken up into smaller 'chunks' of meaning, and you will find the paragraph much easier to read.

> Let me see: / that would be four thousand miles down, / I think—' / (for, you see, / Alice had learnt several things of this sort / in her lessons / in the schoolroom, / and though this was not a VERY good opportunity for showing off her knowledge, / as there was no one to listen to her, / still it was good practice to say it over) / '—yes, / that's about the right distance— / but then I wonder what Latitude or Longitude I've got to?' / (Alice had no idea what Latitude was, / or Longitude either, / but thought they were nice grand words to say.)

3 Now you have a go with the following paragraph. Place a slash (/) between the **main ideas** in each sentence.

> 'I wonder if I shall fall right *THROUGH* the earth! How funny it'll seem to come out among the people that walk with their heads downward! The Antipathies, I think—' (she was rather glad there was no one listening, this time, as it didn't sound at all the right word) '—but I shall have to ask them what the name of the country is, you know. Please, Ma'am, is this New Zealand or Australia?' (and she tried to curtsey as she spoke—fancy *CURTSEYING* as you're falling through the air! Do you think you could manage it?) 'And what an ignorant little girl she'll think me for asking! No, it'll never do to ask: perhaps I shall see it written up somewhere.'

Work on words

Adverbs

An **adverb** can modify (alter/change) a verb, an adjective, another adverb, a phrase or a clause. An adverb points to **manner**, **time**, **place**, **cause** or **degree**, and answers questions such as *how*, *when*, *where*, *why* and *how much*.

While most adverbs end in *ly*, an adverb doesn't always end in *ly* and can be found in various places within the sentence.

1 Review your knowledge of adverbs. Place the following **adverbs** in the sentences below.

anywhere rarely so often there surprisingly

a The student ___eagerly___ anticipated the ball as it was thrown at him.

b The neighbours ______________ take turns taking lunch to the elderly woman's home.

c ______________ she could work faster, the teacher purchased a new computer.

d The tenant instructed the removalists to place the table ______________.

e We ______________ go on holidays, only once a year.

f After living all over the world, I now feel I could live ______________.

g I felt ______________ well, despite getting caught in the sudden rainfall.

2 Circle the **adverbs** in these examples from *Alice's Adventures in Wonderland.* The verbs have been identified to help you.

a 'In another moment down **went** Alice' (one adverb)

b 'The rabbit-hole **went** straight … and then **dipped** suddenly' (two adverbs)

c 'but when the Rabbit actually **took** a watch out of its waistcoat pocket, … and then **hurried** on' (two adverbs)

d 'I wonder if I **shall fall** right *THROUGH* the earth!' (two adverbs)

e 'Either the well **was** very deep, or she **fell** very slowly, for she **had** plenty of time as she **went** down' (four adverbs)

Spotlight on language

Direct and indirect speech

Writers often have to give information about what people say or think in narrative texts. In order to do this they can use direct or indirect speech.

Direct speech is also known as quoted speech and is saying exactly what someone has said. The exact words that someone has spoken appear within quotation marks ('…').

For example: The teacher said, 'Today we will be examining direct speech'.

Indirect speech is also known as reported speech. Indirect speech doesn't use quotation marks to enclose what the person has said and it doesn't have to be word for word (exact).

For example: The teacher said that today we would be examining direct speech.

When using indirect speech, the **tense usually changes**. This is because when we use indirect speech, we are usually talking about something that has already happened. The verbs therefore have to be changed from the present tense to the past tense. The **order of words** in the indirect speech form is often different to the order in the direct speech form, especially if the direct speech is a question.

For example: Suri asked, 'What**'s** the time?' (present tense)
→ Suri asked what the time **was**. (past tense)

1 Insert the correct verb in these examples of **direct speech** (present tense) and **indirect speech** (past tense). The first one has been done for you.

a 'I ____am____ going to the shops', she said.
She said she ____was____ going to the shops.

b Daniel replied, 'I'm not putting up with these conditions any longer'.
Daniel said he ________ not going to put up with these conditions any longer.

c 'The sofa ________ very large', said Emile. 'I hope it will fit.'
Emile said the sofa ________ very large.

d 'I want to go with you now', said Lily.
Lily said that she ________ to go with you now.

e 'What do you need to buy?' inquired Mum.
Mum wondered what I ________.

Note: In *Alice's Adventures in Wonderland,* Alice often uses the verb *shall.* **Shall** is very similar in meaning to **will**. Although still used in modern English, it can create an old-fashioned and 'proper' effect. As *shall* is derived from the Old English *sceal* meaning 'must', it also creates a formal English tone to the story.

When changing direct speech into indirect speech, the verb **shall** changes to **should**.

For example:

Direct speech: The White Rabbit said, 'I **shall** be late'.

Indirect speech: The White Rabbit said that he **should** be late.

2 Change these examples from *Alice's Adventures in Wonderland* from **direct speech** into **indirect speech**. The first one has been done for you.

a '… and what **is** the use of a book', thought Alice, 'without pictures or conversation?'
Alice wondered what the use of a book was without pictures or conversation.

b 'I **shall** think nothing of tumbling down stairs!'
Alice exclaimed that she ________ think nothing of tumbling down stairs.

c 'I wonder how many miles **I've** fallen by this time?' she said aloud.
Alice wondered how many miles she ________ fallen this time.

d 'I wonder if I **shall** fall right THROUGH the earth!'
Alice wondered if she ________________.

e '... perhaps I **shall** see it written up somewhere.'

Alice questioned whether she ______________________________.

f '... but I **shall** have to ask them what the name of the country is'

Alice said that she ______________________________.

Extend your skills

Alice's Adventures in Wonderland was written in 1865 in Victorian England. As a result, the language is quite formal and at times outdated. The author uses complex sentences that create descriptiveness as well as old-fashioned verbs like *shall*, and these add to the text's quaintness and old-world feeling.

Rewrite the opening two paragraphs; however, change and modernise the setting, characters and dialogue to the present world. The words Alice speaks and the things she does should be consistent with how a young girl would speak and act today, and not during Victorian England.

UNIT NINE

Cartoons

Before you read

It's always a good idea to glance quickly at a text before you read it in detail. This **previewing** is useful even if the text is quite short. Previewing allows you to make forecasts or predictions about what you are going to read. This then makes your reading easier and gives you a reason to continue to read, as you confirm or discard your predictions.

Take a brief look for **no more than 3 seconds** at the following images and words. What topic or subject do you think this cartoon is focusing on?

___

___

___

___

___

The Big Boss

Source: sangrea.net

Test your understanding

1 Tick (✓) the best answer. The cartoon's main character is a CEO. What do you think this stands for?

a Catholic Education Office ______

b Chief Executive Officer ______

c Chief Electoral Officer ______

d Chief Ethics Officer ______

2 Tick (✓) the best answer. Cartoonists create cartoons for different purposes. What do you think is the purpose of this cartoon?

a to tell a funny story ______

b to express an opinion on society ______

c to make fun of a particular person ______

d to entertain ______

e to express a political opinion ______

3 Explain why you chose this answer.

____

____

____

4 Tick (✓) the best answer. One of the following is the correct title for this cartoon.

- **a** Business ______
- **b** Perspective ______
- **c** Greed Is Good ______
- **d** Day at the Office ______

5 Why did you choose this title?

____

____

6 Tick (✓) the correct answer. What is the cartoon's main setting?

- **a** outer space ______
- **b** an office building ______
- **c** an office ______
- **d** a space station ______

7 Tick (✓) the ideas below that you think the cartoonist is communicating. There may be more than one.

- **a** ______ There is always another company that is bigger than yours.
- **b** ______ Most people are important.
- **c** ______ People often don't consider their place in the wider world.
- **d** ______ We are all fairly insignificant, no matter how important we may feel we are.
- **e** ______ The earth looks really small from outer space.

8 Cartoonists are very clever at communicating information using very simple lines and pen strokes. Looking at the character in Image 1, circle three of the following words that best describe him. You may need a dictionary to check the in meaning.

friendly	ambitious	smug	self-important	arrogant	majestic

9 What do the character's words, 'Hey, this is ok. I'm really, really, really important!' reveal about his personality?

____

____

10 Tick (✓) the correct answer. In Image 3, what do you notice about Big Co Pty Ltd?

- **a** It's a big company. ______
- **b** It's the biggest company on the block. ______
- **c** The company next door is actually bigger. ______
- **d** The man in the office has moved. ______

11 What do you think is the most important idea or feature of this cartoon?

____

____

____

Boost your reading skills

Reading and understanding cartoons

Cartoons can sometimes force us to look at our behaviour as a society through their messages. Some cartoonists laugh at or expose people, events or attitudes which they feel society needs to think about.

Three concepts that are important to understanding cartoons are **tone**, **values** and **context**.

Tone is the cartoonist's attitude—the position, or stance—that the cartoonist takes in order to present his or her ideas. Tone may be described as **positive**, **negative** or **neutral**. An example of a neutrally toned text is a Wikipedia page, which is formal, serious and knowledgeable.

We use tone in our everyday life. As an exercise to think about how you use tone, look at the following phrase and say it in the different ways listed. You will see how the meaning changes with the tone used:

'Close the door, Alexander.'

This simple sentence can be commanding, secretive, loving, playful or exasperated—depending on how you say it.

1 **a** Place the following words into their correct category to describe **tone**. The first row has been done for you.

delighted	depressed	serious	pleasant	sympathetic	solemn	spiteful
formal	fearful	sarcastic	pleased	cheerful	excited	
loving	questioning	hopeful	annoyed	outraged	knowledgeable	

Positive	**Neutral**	**Negative**
delighted	formal	depressed

b Circle three words that best reflect the **tone** of the cartoon at the start of the unit.

thoughtful   bored   proud   amazed   critical   questioning

Values are the ideas or beliefs that a person or group considers important.
For example: honesty, integrity, sharing, morals, truth, honour, reliability, decency.

2 Place a tick (✓) next to the following **values** you believe the cartoon communicates.

a Businesses should have more integrity. ______

b Businesses are free to be dishonest. ______

c Businesses should be more aware of the 'big picture'. ______

d It's accepted for businesses to be self-serving and selfish. ______

e It's a mistake to believe that you are very important. ______

3 Values can change over time and are influenced by society's expectations and attitudes at particular points in time. Underline the following **values** that you believe reflect the attitudes and feelings of a modern society.

a The environment needs protecting.

b Girls should learn how to cook and clean.

c Women can be leaders.

d It's ok for boys to cry.

e It's important to recycle.

f People should just drive everywhere.

g Smoking is not dangerous.

Context relates to the different personal, social, cultural and historical factors that influence meaning in a text.

4 Circle the correct answer.

a Where is the cartoon set?	Australia	Asia	Africa
b What is the specific location?	place of business	school	Earth
c When is the cartoon set?	the past	the present	the future
d What is the context of the cartoon?	modern old-fashioned	ancient historical	

Work on words

Cartoon techniques

All cartoonists have access to a collection of tools and **techniques** that help them get their point across. Understanding these techniques and the words to describe them will help you interpret and write about the **purpose** and **effect** of **cartoons**.

1 Fill in the missing word(s) to show your **understanding** of the following terms. The first one has been done for you.

doodle	length of shot	punctuation	pun
caption	dialogue	body language	exaggeration
caricatures	facial expressions	costume	speech bubbles

a A ____doodle____ is a rough drawing, sometimes made absentmindedly.

b Speech balloons, also known as ____________, are a graphic feature used most commonly in comic books to show what a character is saying.

c The dress, suit, clothing, garb or attire of a character is known as their ____________.

d A ____________ is a title or brief explanation attached to an article, illustration or poster.

e Conversation between two or more people as a feature of a cartoon is known as ____________.

f A ____________, also known as a 'play on words', makes a joke exploiting the many possible meanings of a word.

g A picture called a ____________ exaggerates people or things for comic and humorous effect.

h The marks, such as full stops, commas and parentheses, used in writing to separate sentences and to clarify meaning are called ____________.

i ____________ are the feelings and thoughts expressed on a person's face.

j To overstate or represent something as greater is known as ____________ and may be communicated through both words and pictures.

k ____________ is the process of communicating non-verbally through gestures and movements.

l When describing shots, ____________ is used to indicate the amount of subject matter contained within a frame and how far away the audience is from the subject. Examples are close-up, medium shot, long shot and extreme long shot.

2 Now place the terms from Question 1 under their correct category. (Note: one of them appears in both columns.)

doodle	length of shot	punctuation	pun
caption	dialogue	body language	exaggeration
caricatures	facial expressions	costume	thought bubbles

Words associated with pictures/images	Words associated with language
doodles	caption

3 In the table you completed for Question 2, place a tick (✓) next to the words that you think are used by the given cartoon.

Cartoon purposes

A cartoon's purpose might be to:

- **entertain** and make us laugh
- **raise ideas** about issues such as the environment
- **satirise** (send-up, ridicule, laugh at) people, or ideas, such as politicians
- **imitate** and **mock** human weaknesses, such as greed and selfishness.

The following terms will help you understand and talk about a cartoon's **purpose**.

- **expose**—uncover and disclose (e.g. The cartoon **exposes** ideas about celebrities and vanity.)

- **insight**—an understanding of something (e.g. The audience gained an **insight** into the modern world.)
- **irony**—the meaning of words and images is different to the stated one (e.g. The contrasting images in the cartoon allow us to appreciate the **irony** of the businessman's words.)
- **confront**—address an issue or problem (e.g. The issues exposed by the cartoon were designed to **confront** the audience.)
- **mock**—ridicule or make fun of a person or thing (e.g. The cartoonist aims to **mock** using a ridiculing tone.)
- **ridiculous**—absurd or laughable (e.g. The cartoonist has made that politician appear **ridiculous**.)
- **sarcasm**—a mocking use of words that mean the opposite to what is said (e.g. The cartoonist uses **sarcasm** when she tells us that the businessman thinks he is '... really, really important'.)
- **satire**—the use of mocking or exaggerated humour to ridicule faults or vices (e.g. The cartoon contains elements of **satire** as it uses humour to force the audience to feel uncomfortable about aspects of their behaviour.)

4 Complete the following sentences using words from the list of purposes.

A cartoon is a simple drawing that often uses ____________________. It may or may not contain a caption. A cartoonist's purpose is to ____________________ issues in society and influence public opinion. The cartoonist's purpose may be to entertain us and make us laugh. Or their purpose may be more serious, through their use of ____________________. They may be sending an important message such as a social or political comment or criticism. The cartoonist in the text at the start of the unit uses words and pictures to reveal her ____________________ towards big business. The cartoonist makes businesses appear ____________________ in order to give an ____________________ into aspects of our modern society.

Spotlight on language

Exaggeration and irony

We have looked already at the techniques cartoonists use to get their message across and to make their readers laugh. Here we look again at two of those techniques—**exaggeration** and **irony**.

Exaggeration is where cartoonists overstate or make obvious the physical appearance of people or things in order to highlight an idea.

For example: the cartoonist might make a parent in a cartoon look ridiculously tall next to a small child to highlight the difference in their power and status.

1 **a** Find examples of both words and pictures from the cartoon that communicate that the main character is a business manager in an office setting.

____

____

____

b Are any of these words and pictures an **exaggeration**? If yes, which ones?

______

______

c Tick (✓) two of the following. Why do you think the cartoonist has **exaggerated** the words and physical appearance of the business manager?

i to make him appear slightly ridiculous ______

ii to show that all business managers look like this ______

iii to make a point about the personality of the manager ______

iv to make you feel sorry for him ______

Irony in its most basic form is where the meaning of a word, image or action is the opposite of, or different from, the stated one.

For example: someone saying, 'I just love rain' as they sit huddled under umbrellas watching a football game.

Another form of irony is often used in creative texts such as cartoons. This is sometimes called **dramatic irony**. It basically means that we, the audience, know more than the characters in the text know.

For example: in Shakespeare's *Romeo and Juliet*, the main characters in the play, including Romeo, believe Juliet to be dead, but the audience knows she only took a sleeping potion.

Cartoonists often use irony to express their opinion on an issue. The cartoonist of *The Big Boss* has used **contrasting distances** to create irony within the cartoon. The **length of the shot** has been used to particular effect to help make the main point of the cartoon.

2 Label each row in the cartoon close-up, medium shot, long shot or extreme long shot.

Row 1 ______ Row 2 ______ Row 3 ______ Row 4 ______

3 Tick (✓) the correct answer. Which of the following statements best explains the use of **irony** in the cartoon?

a We see how important the office and the CEO are, but the businessman does not. ______

b We see how big the world is but the CEO does not. ______

c We see how small the office and the CEO are, but the businessman does not. ______

d We see and understand why the CEO and his job are so important. ______

4 Is the first frame (or image) of the cartoon an example of the ways things often are in life or the ways things should be? Explain your answer.

______

______

5 The sixth frame of the cartoon communicates the truth, or reality, of our lives. What is this truth or reality? Explain your answer.

______

______

______

Extend your skills

Find a cartoon to analyse in a newspaper or on the internet and then fill in the table.

List the things or people you see in the cartoon.	
What is the cartoon title?	
Write down any important numbers that appear in the cartoon.	
Describe the action taking place in the cartoon.	
Which of the objects on your list are symbols?	
What do you think each symbol means?	
Which words or phrases in the cartoon appear to be the most important? Why do you think so?	
Explain the message of the cartoon.	
Who in society would agree/ disagree with the cartoon's message? Why?	

Fact sheet

Before you read

Looking at headlines, subheadings and visuals before you read a text is a good **previewing** technique. It will help you understand the content and structure of what you are going to read.

1 Tick (✓) the best answer. Read the headline *Eat more fruit and vegies* and look at the picture *5 ways to a healthy lifestyle.* Look at the name of the website and the address, and at the section headings. Which statement best summarises what you think this fact sheet will be about?

- **a** exercise ideas for young people ______
- **b** what it means to eat well ______
- **c** eating fruit and vegetables as part of a healthy lifestyle for young people ______
- **d** information about how good fruit and vegetables are for you ______

2 Who do you think this fact sheet is written for?

____

Eat more fruit and vegies

www.healthykids.nsw.gov.au

Eat more fruit and vegies

Did you know?

★ 56% of primary and 80% of secondary school students do not eat the recommended daily amount of vegetables.

★ Research shows that watching a lot of TV is associated with children and teenagers drinking more soft drink and not eating enough fruit and vegetables.

★ Fruit and vegetables are a great source of vitamins, minerals and dietary fibre.

★ Eating fruit and vegetables every day helps children and teenagers grow and develop, boosts their vitality and can reduce the risk of many chronic diseases - such as heart disease, high blood pressure, some forms of cancer and being overweight or obese.

How many serves do kids and teens need?

All of us need to eat a variety of different coloured fruit and vegies every day – both raw and cooked. The recommended daily amount for kids and teens depends on their age, appetite and activity levels – see table below.

Age *(years)*	Fruit *(serves/day*)*		Vegies *(serves/day^)*	
	girls	boys	girls	boys
2-3	1	1	2½	2½
4-8	1½	1½	4½	4½
9-11	2	2	5	5
12-18	2	2	5	5½

**One serve of fruit is 150 grams (equal to 1 medium-sized apple; 2 smaller pieces (e.g. apricots); 1 cup of canned or chopped fruit; ½ cup (125ml) 99% unsweetened fruit juice; or 1½ tablespoons dried fruit).*

^One serve of vegetables is 75 grams (equal to ½ cup cooked vegetables; ½ medium potato; 1 cup of salad vegetables; or ½ cup cooked legumes (dried beans, peas or lentils)

Fresh fruit is a better choice than juice

While whole fruit contains some natural sugars that make it taste sweet, it also has lots of vitamins, minerals and fibre, which makes it more filling and nutritious than a glass of fruit juice.

One small glass of juice provides a child's recommended daily amount of vitamin C. Unfortunately, many children regularly drink large amounts of juice and this can contribute to them putting on excess weight.

"Children may need to try new fruits and vegies up to 10 times before they accept them"

continues over the page ▶

How to help kids and teens eat more fruit and vegies

Eating more fruit and vegies every day can sometimes be a struggle. However, research shows that we're more likely to do so if they're available and ready to eat.

Children may need to try new fruits and vegies up to 10 times before they accept them. So stay patient and keep offering them. It can also help to prepare and serve them in different and creative ways.

Some ideas to try:

- Involve the whole family in choosing and preparing fruit and vegies.
- Select fruit and vegies that are in season – they taste better and are usually cheaper.
- Keep a bowl of fresh fruit in the home.
- Be creative in how you prepare and serve fruit and vegies, such as raw, sliced, grated, microwaved, mashed or baked; serve different coloured fruit and vegies or use different serving plates or bowls.
- Include fruit and vegies in every meal. For example, add chopped, grated or pureed vegies to pasta sauces, meat burgers, frittatas, stir-fries and soups, and add fruit to breakfast cereal.
- Snack on fruit and vegies. Try corn on the cob; jacket potato topped with reduced fat cheese; plain popcorn (unbuttered and without sugar or salt coating); chopped vegies with salsa, hummus or yoghurt dips; stewed fruit; fruit crumble; frozen fruit; or muffins made with fruit or vegies.
- Try different fruits or vegies on your toast – banana, mushrooms or tomatoes.
- Add chopped or pureed fruit to plain yoghurts.
- Make a fruit smoothie with fresh, frozen or canned (in natural or unsweetened juice) fruit; blend it with reduced fat milk and yoghurt.
- Chop up some fruit or vegie sticks for the lunchbox.
- In summer, freeze fruit on a skewer (or mix with yoghurt before freezing) for a refreshing snack.
- Make fruit-based desserts (such as fruit crumble or baked, poached or stewed fruit) and serve with reduced fat custard.
- Have fresh fruit available at all times as a convenient snack – keep the fruit bowl full and have diced fruit in a container in the fridge.

For more information and ideas on healthy eating and physical activity, go to www.healthykids.nsw.gov.au

Source: Healthy Kids Website (2013). An initiative of NSW Ministry of Health; NSW Department of Education and Communities and the Heart Foundation. www.healthykids.nsw.gov.au

Test your understanding

1 Mark the following statements as True (T) or False (F).

- **a** The fact sheet wants kids to eat more fruit and vegetables. ______
- **b** Only 60% of children eat the correct amount of vegetables every day. ______
- **c** Watching a lot of TV contributes to an unhealthy lifestyle. ______
- **d** Water is a better choice of drink than juice. ______
- **e** Being overweight is not a real problem for young people. ______
- **f** Fruit juice should be chosen over a piece of fruit. ______
- **g** It could take up to ten tastes of a fruit or vegetable to accept it into your diet. ______

2 Tick (✓) the best answer. The fourth point in the opening list of the fact sheet outlines the benefits of eating fruit and vegies every day. Which statement best summarises these benefits?

- **a** Fruit and vegies help young people grow, live with energy and avoid illness. ______
- **b** Fruit and vegetables are a great source of fibre and reduce heart disease. ______
- **c** Close to 60% of children do not eat the recommended daily amount of fruit and vegies. ______
- **d** Fruit and vegies encourage young people to turn off the TV and do more exercise. ______

3 Tick (✓) the correct answer. Why is fresh fruit a better choice than juice, according to the fact sheet?

- **a** Whole fruit contains natural sugars. ______
- **b** Fruit contains vitamin C. ______
- **c** A whole piece of fruit is more filling and nutritious. ______
- **d** Fresh fruit tastes sweet. ______

4 Tick (✓) the correct answer. In the sentence 'Eating fruit and vegetables boosts children's vitality', which word could replace *boosts*?

- **a** supports ______
- **b** increases ______
- **c** declines ______
- **d** spreads ______

5 The article tells us that eating fruit and vegetables can be a struggle for some young people. Why do you think this is?

____

____

____

6 Tick (✓) the correct answer. The section *Some ideas to try* lists different food and cooking ideas. Why have they been included?

a to encourage more cooking with fruit and vegies ______

b to provide information ______

c to promote healthy eating ______

d all of the above ______

Boost your reading skills

Graphic organisers

A **graphic organiser** is a visual text that shows relationships between ideas. Graphic organisers are also sometimes referred to as knowledge maps, concept maps, mind maps or concept diagrams. They can help you make sense of data and interpret information, and are a valuable way for you to reorganise information to show your knowledge and understanding.

The fact sheet uses two examples of graphic organisers to communicate ideas and information. These are a **cycle** and a **table**.

A **cycle** is a graphic organiser used to sequence things that repeatedly cycle, such as the seasons.

1 **a** Underline three of the following topics for which you could use a **cycle organiser**.

- favourite movies
- lifecycle of a butterfly
- how we sleep
- what are stars
- precipitation (rain)

b The fact sheet *Eat more fruit and vegies* uses a **cycle** diagram to show information about five ways to a healthy lifestyle. Why do you think they have they used this style of graphic organiser to present this particular information?

c How many of the *5 ways to a healthy lifestyle* do you follow in your life at the moment?

d Has the **cycle graph** persuaded you to improve your eating and exercise habits? ______
If so, how did it persuade you?

A **table** is a graphic organiser can be used to present or to summarise information. It is especially useful with numerical information.
The fact sheet uses a table (under the title *How many serves do kids and teens need?*) to communicate how many serves of fruit and vegetables kids and teenagers should be eating each day.

Look at the table in the fact sheet and answer these questions.

2 **a** How many serves of fruit per day should an 8- to 11-year-old child consume?

b Tick (✓) the entire age range presented by the table.

i 4–7 ______

ii 4–18 ______

iii 8–11 ______

iv 4–9 ______

c Label the following statements True (T) or False (F).

i Six year olds should eat more fruit than 18 year olds. ______

ii All ages should eat a variety of fruits and vegetables daily. ______

iii There are three main stages of youth presented in the table. ______

iv Four to 7 year olds should eat the same amount of fruit as 8 to 11 year olds. ______

d Think about the amount of fruits and vegetables you eat. Do you eat more or less than the table recommends? ______

e Use the table below to summarise information from the opening paragraph of the fact sheet entitled 'Did you know?' The titles have been provided for you.

Benefits of eating fruit and vegetables	Statistics about fruit and vegetables	Effects of TV on healthy eating habits

Work on words

Technical language

Technical language is language and vocabulary that is special to a **particular trade, profession** or **group**. There are special terms and words that relate to science, art, music, cooking, politics and just about any topic. You will often find examples of technical language when reading. If the meaning of the word is not clear, look at the rest of the sentence to provide some clues to the unfamiliar words.

Technical language can sometimes be referred to as 'jargon'. The term *jargon* has some negative associations, however, because it is technical language that may be used to exclude people from the group who are using it.

1 Fill in the following table, sorting the **technical language** examples according to where they are used. Some have been done for you.

CYA	HSC	lower house	democracy	test tube
onstitution	BTW	microscope	attacker	elements
back pass	ground beans	soy mocha chino	PDHPE	
irrigate	left wing	mouse	landscaping	
astronomy	LOL	gifted and talented	curriculum	

Location	Jargon
school	HSC, curriculum
gardeners	irrigate
politicians	lower house
the Internet	
cafes	
science	microscope
football	

The fact sheet uses **technical language** related to diets and healthy eating. It does this in order to educate readers about the topic. Technical language in the fact sheet creates a **factual** and **reliable tone**, and as a result it makes the information appear knowledgeable and trustworthy.

2 The following words are taken from the fact sheet. Circle the words you think are **technical language** related to the topic of healthy eating.

vitamins	children	heart disease	struggle	source
TV	obese	taste	raw	minerals
dietary fibre	recommended daily amount			

3 Sometimes words that are very common in everyday life have a specific technical meaning in special situations. Circle the best two definitions to show your understanding of the following examples in **bold** of **technical language** from the fact sheet. The first one has been done for you.

- **a** In NSW, close to 60% of children do not eat the **recommended** (advised/admired/suggested) daily amount of vegetables.
- **b** Fruit and vegetables are a great source of vitamins, minerals and **dietary** (nutritious/nourishing/unwholesome) fibre.
- **c** Eating fruit and vegetables every day helps children and teenagers ... reduce the risk of many **chronic** (chaotic/enduring/long-lasting) diseases.
- **d** While whole fruit contains some **natural** (pure/artificial/unprocessed) sugars that make it taste sweet, it also has lots of vitamins, minerals and fibre which make it more filling and nutritious.
- **e** ... many children regularly drink large amounts of juice and this can contribute to them putting on **excess** (deficiency/oversupply/surplus) weight.
- **f** The recommended daily amount for kids and teens depends on their age, **appetite** (aversion/inclination/craving) and activity levels.

Spotlight on language

Language of instruction

Instructions are guidelines that show people how to perform a particular task. The second page of the fact sheet entitled *How to help kids and teens eat more fruit and vegies: Some ideas to try* is a set of instructions that focus on providing different and interesting food ideas.

1 Complete the following sentence by ticking (✓) one of the following endings.

The main purpose of the set of instructions is to

- **a** help young people become familiar with recipes. ______
- **b** provide more information about different types of fruit and vegetables. ______
- **c** outline skills so that young people can become better cooks. ______
- **d** provide different and interesting food ideas so that young people will eat a greater variety and volume of fruits and vegetables. ______

2 The table focuses on different features of **instructions**. Fill it in after looking at the section of the fact sheet called *How to help kids and teens eat more fruit and vegies: Some ideas to try*.

Does the instruction in the fact sheet:	**Yes (✓)**	**No (✓)**	**Example**
✱ start with an aim or goal?	✓		Information under *How to help kids and teens eat more fruit and vegies* provides the purpose/objective for the following recipe ideas.
✱ provide a list of what tools are needed?		✓	
✱ provide information on how to do something? (method)			
✱ include a diagram or picture?			
✱ use clear and brief vocabulary?			
✱ use the present tense?			
✱ use action verbs (e.g. *take*, *put* or *mix*)?			
✱ organise information by using bullet points?			

3 Based on your findings in the table, are the fact sheet's **instructions** on how to help kids and teens eat more fruit and vegies effective and well written?

____

Why/Why not?

____

____

____

____

Extend your skills

A **KWL** chart allows you to record what you already **knew** (**K**) about a topic, what you **want** (**W**) to learn more about and a place to record what you have actually **learnt** (**L**).

Fill in the following **KWL** chart based on your reading of the *Eat more fruit and vegies* fact sheet.

K— What I know	**W—What I want to know**	**L—What I learned**
Write what you already knew about the topic before reading the fact sheet.	After reading it, what would you like to find out more about?	What have you learned about the topic of healthy lifestyles for kids?

UNIT ELEVEN

Biography

Before you read

Thinking about what you know of the subject of a text and then **skimming** to get an overview are good pre-reading strategies when reading any text.

1 Do you know who David Beckham is?

____

What have you heard, seen or read about him?

____

____

____

2 Skim the following text for 60 seconds and then put a tick (✓) next to the topics you saw mentioned, without looking back.

a David Beckham's early childhood ______

b David Beckham's history with Manchester United ______

c David Beckham's family life with wife and children ______

d Examples of difficulties in David Beckham's career ______

David Beckham biography

Sports Articles | July 17, 2007

I really thought I knew everything there is about the midfielder, but reading a David Beckham biography I found out more about the man behind the superstar. That's why I decided to write my own biography of David Beckham—to share with you the player behind the million-dollar endorsements.

Manchester United

David Beckham's story starts out near London, where he was born to a family of Manchester United fans. Despite being so close to clubs like West Ham United, Arsenal or Chelsea, Beckham's aim was always the Red Devils club. As luck would have it, on his fourteenth birthday, he was taken in the Manchester youth program, and he even starred next to the senior team … as a mascot.

Just 4 years later, he went on to play for Sir Alex Ferguson's senior squad, but his performance still needed fine tuning, so he was loaned to Preston North End for a year, returning to Manchester with some match experience. He quickly gained his place in the squad, despite his young age and became one of Manchester's most preeminent players during the following decade.

His most successful season with Manchester is undoubtedly 1999, when the club achieved the Treble (League, Cup and Champions League in the same season) and with David Beckham playing soccer like never before.

It's around then that he 'trademarked' his famous free kicks and crosses and seeing some footage of David Beckham in action during that period will shed all doubts as to whether or not his superstar status has a solid basis in his playing style, or just his good looks.

1998 World Cup Incident

His career did have a few rough moments, the most notable one being in 1998 with the English national side, at that year's World Cup. In the Second Round, where England would play Argentina, Beckham was taunted by Argentinean midfielder Diego Simeone and he responded with a swing towards the player, which earned him a red card for bad behaviour on the pitch.

With England losing the match and being knocked out of the tournament, all blame fell on David Beckham, as the English newspapers put him against the wall and fired up some poisonous articles. Any other player would have stayed low, or even quit soccer, but David Beckham's ambition brought him back to the top. His performance with Manchester the following year earned him back the respect of his fans and the entire world.

Real Madrid

By the time David Beckham moved to Real Madrid in 2003, he was already a well-known star on the international stage. In his four years with the Madrid club he managed to win the Spanish league once, but his performance was deemed poorer than when he was playing at Manchester. Many attributed this loss of form due to the new system found at Real and the fact that at Madrid he wasn't the 'star' of the team anymore, since he was playing next to other internationally famous soccer players like Zinedine Zidane, Raul or Roberto Carlos.

Los Angeles Galaxy

Moving to play in the United States for the Los Angeles Galaxy as of 2007 earned him one of the biggest contracts in the history of soccer and it was an offer David couldn't have refused, despite the fact that the soccer level in the United States is not as high as the one practiced in Spain.

Source: Free Articles from ArticlesFactory.com

Test your understanding

Tick (✓) the correct answer for each of the following questions.

1 What is a biography?

- **a** a made-up story about someone's life ______
- **b** the life story of the author ______
- **c** the true story of someone's life ______
- **d** a report ______

2 Manchester United, Real Madrid and Los Angeles Galaxy are examples of

- **a** countries.
- **b** holiday destinations. ______
- **c** soccer players. ______
- **d** soccer teams. ______

3 A midfielder is a player whose usual position is in the midfield (in the middle of the pitch). In paragraph 1, why has Beckham been referred to as *the* midfielder, and not *a* midfielder?

- **a** The biographer really likes David Beckham. ______
- **b** He is the only midfielder. ______
- **c** The article is referring to any midfielder. ______
- **d** This is the position for which David Beckham is recognised. ______

4 Which quote from the biography best shows an opinion of David Beckham?

a David Beckham's story starts out near London. ______

b His most successful season with Manchester is undoubtedly 1999. ______

c His career did have a few rough moments. ______

d The soccer level in the United States is not as high as the one practiced in Spain. ______

5 In the line '... became one of Manchester's most preeminent players', *preeminent* could be replaced with

a developing. ______

b outstanding. ______

c well-known. ______

d disliked. ______

6 Number these events from David Beckham's life and career in the correct order from 1 to 5.

a ______ has most successful season with Manchester in 1999

b ______ moves to America to play for Los Angeles *Galaxy*

c ______ is born to a family of Manchester United fans

d ______ earns a red card for swinging at a player

e ______ moved to play for Real Madrid in 2003

7 The following are events from David Beckham's life. Write if they are positive (*P*) or negative (*N*).

a Many attributed this loss of form due to the new system found at Real. ______

b He quickly gained his place in the squad, despite his young age. ______

c ... but his performance was deemed poorer than what he was playing at Manchester ______

d ... he even starred next to the senior team ... as a mascot ______

e With England losing the match and being knocked out of the tournament, all blame fell on David Beckham. ______

8 What is your overall impression of/feelings about David Beckham after reading this biography of his life and career?

____

____

____

____

____

____

____

Boost your reading skills

Using context clues to work out meanings

The **meaning** of a word can often be worked out by looking at its **context** (situation) within the sentence.

For example: Imran was pleased that his ideas **facilitated**, rather than delayed, the situation and assisted the group to reach a decision.

You may work out the meaning of *facilitated* by using the meaning of other words in the sentence. If you know the meaning of *delayed*, which is 'to be stopped or held up', then the sentence tells you that Imran's ideas did *not* have this effect. *Facilitated* is the antonym (opposite) of *delayed* and means 'enabled, helped or made easy'. Also, Imran is *pleased*, which communicates that the word *facilitated* may have a positive meaning.

1 Look at each sentence and try to work out the **meaning** of the underlined word.

a After being naughty, Isabel redeemed herself by washing the dishes for mum.

Redeemed means ______________________

b Ming loathed tennis and couldn't wait for the match to be over.

Loathed means ______________________

c Toula got caught in the storm and her appearance was dishevelled.

Dishevelled means ______________________

d The car was obstructed by the large truck and couldn't drive down the road.

Obstructed means ______________________

e Paula found the book enchanting and couldn't wait to share it with her friends.

Enchanting means ______________________

2 Look at the examples from the David Beckham biography. Read the entire sentence to help you work out the **meaning** of the italicised word. Underline the section of the sentence that gave you a clue.

a That's why I decided to write my own biography of David Beckham—to share with you the player behind the million-dollar endorsements.

What is an *endorsement*? This is when an athlete is highly paid to promote a product.

b Just 4 years later, he went on to play for Sir Alex Ferguson's senior squad, but his performance still needed fine tuning.

What is *fine-tuning*? ______________________

____

c His career did have a few rough moments, the most notable one being in 1998 with the English national side …

What does *notable* mean? ______________________

____

d Beckham was taunted by Argentinean midfielder Diego Simeone and he responded with a swing towards the player.

What does *taunted* mean? ______________________________

____

e With England losing the match and being knocked out of the tournament, all blame fell on David Beckham …

What does *knocked out* mean? ______________________________

____

f … the English newspapers put him against the wall and fired up some poisonous articles.

What does *poisonous* mean in this sentence? ______________________________

____

Work on words

Language of opinion in biographies

The biographer's **choice of language** can **influence** the way the reader views the person being written about in a biography. If a biographer approves of a person or event they will use positive or favourable language. For instance, describing a person as *ambitious* presents a more favourable image than describing them as *pushy* or *ruthless*.

1 Match each **positive** word on the left to the **negative** equivalent on the right.

a young	risk-taking
b brave	common
c thrifty	naive
d eccentric	old-fashioned
e famous	stingy
f popular	notorious
g antique	weird

2 The following words show the author's **attitude** towards his subject, David Beckham.

star preeminent ambitious respect distinguished gained

On the basis of this language, how would you describe the author's attitude towards David Beckham?

____

____

____

3 The following statements are from the David Beckham biography. Next to each positive bracketed word, find a less favourable (negative) option.

problematic notorious vanity obedience undeveloped ruthlessness infamous celebrity

a Any other player would have stayed low, or even quit soccer, but David Beckham's (ambition) ______________ brought him back to the top.

b His career did have a few (rough) ______________ moments.

c He quickly gained his place in the squad, despite his (young) ______________ age and became one of Manchester's most (preeminent) ______________ players during the following decade.

d It's around then that he 'trademarked' his (famous) ______________ free kicks and crosses and seeing some footage of David Beckham in action during that period will shed all doubts as to whether or not his (superstar) ______________ status has a solid basis in his playing style, or just his (good looks) ______________.

Spotlight on language

Fact or opinion?

A biography is a text containing information that is both fact and opinion. This is because it contains information about a person's life that can be proved, and it also contains the writer's opinions and feelings towards the person they are writing the biography on.

A **fact** is a statement that can be proved true or false. It can be supported by evidence. When thinking about facts, ask yourself the following.

- Can I prove and verify that the idea is correct?
- Can the information be checked in some way?

If your answer to both of these questions is yes, the statement is a fact.

An **opinion** is what a person thinks or believes. If a statement uses opinion words such as nicest, always, never, all, none, most, least, greatest, best and worst, then it most likely is an opinion because it represents someone's personal opinions and feelings instead of fact. These ideas are hard to prove as they mean something different to everyone involved.

1 Look at the following statements and mark them as either fact or opinion. If they can be proved« write *F* for **fact**. If they use opinion words, or represent feelings, write *O* for **opinion**.

a Children always tell the truth. ______

b Roger Federer is the greatest tennis player of all time. ______

c The earth is made up of five oceans. ______

d All Australians enjoy a good barbeque. ______

e In 1777, Captain Cook visited the Cook Islands, New Zealand and Tasmania. ______

f A salad that has no dressing contains fewer calories. ______

2 For the following examples, say whether they are **fact** (F) or **opinion** (O). Underline the word(s) that support your answer. The first one has been done for you.

- **a** Sailing is an exciting sport. O
- **b** Every teenager has the right to learn to drive. ______
- **c** The cost of living is increasing. ______
- **d** Green is a relaxing colour. ______
- **e** Tasmania is a lovely holiday destination. ______

3 Mark these examples from the David Beckham biography as either **fact** (F) or **opinion** (O). The first one has been done for you.

- **a** Just 4 years later, he went on to play for Sir Alex Ferguson's senior squad … F
- **b** By the time David Beckham moved to Real Madrid in 2003, he was already a well-known star on the international stage. ______
- **c** His most successful season with Manchester is undoubtedly 1999 … ______
- **d** Any other player would have stayed low, or even quit soccer, but David Beckham's ambition brought him back to the top. ______
- **e** His performance with Manchester the following year earned him back the respect of his fans and the entire world. ______
- **f** … he responded with a swing towards the player, which earned him a red card for bad behaviour on the pitch. ______

Extend your skills

1 Write a short biography of someone you know. This could be a classmate or a family member. Start with the following questions.

- Where and when were you born?
- Describe the members of your immediate family.
- Describe an exciting, joyful or unhappy event that occurred to you.
- What are your hopes for your future?

2 Your biography should use examples of positive or negative language that reflect your **attitude** towards your subject. It should also contain a mix of fact and opinion, depending on the type of information you are recording. Write the first paragraph of your biography, using the information you were given from the questions above.

UNIT TWELVE

Advice article

Before you read

An important part of reading is **bringing what you know** about the world to the text you are looking at. It is also a good idea to give the text a general **overview** to get an overall impression before you look at it in more detail.

1 Think of some situations where you have been given advice or have given advice to someone else on buying something. What advice did you give?

____

____

____

2 Read the title and the first paragraph of the article only and look at the image. What do you think this article is going to be about?

____

____

____

Gift ideas for your gamer this holiday season

1 If you aren't a gamer yourself, buying for one can sometimes be a bit overwhelming considering the rapidly evolving technology and the choices in video games. With a few bits of good advice, you can easily find a gift that will delight anyone who enjoys gaming.

2 Keep in mind that gamers are always looking for ways to improve their playing experience. Therefore, there's no such thing as a gamer who has everything. Here are a few ways to find the perfect gift for the video game-lover in your life.

3 Buy them new games based on fan-favourite classic brands. Find a genre that features inherently fun and timelessly cool gameplay. This holiday season, you can find two new offerings from the TRANSFORMERS franchise for gamers of every age, allowing players to assume control of the famous transforming robots.

4 TRANSFORMERS: FALL OF CYBERTRON allows players to experience the most pivotal, post-apocalyptic battles of TRANSFORMERS lore that lead to their famed exodus from their home planet. Great for older teens and adults, the game is a cinematic and immersive action shooter available for PlayStation 3, Xbox 360 and PC.

5 Great for younger fans, TRANSFORMERS PRIME is a family-friendly game based on the popular animated television series of the same name. This one lets players change form and power-up their favourite AUTOBOTS in diverse vistas around the world while cultivating friendships with Jack, Miko and Raf, the human characters from the show. This game is available on Nintendo's Wii U, Wii, 3DS and DS systems.

6 Think about accessories. Gamers can never have enough accessories, from extra controllers to gamer-friendly computer keyboards to 3-D glasses for compatible systems. Do a little fishing for ideas by talking to your recipient (or his or her parents) and see if there's something special to add to their gaming setup.

7 Find official apparel from their favourite game titles or vintage video game T-shirts, which are sure to be a hit especially if your recipient is a bit older and has been a long-time gamer. This is a great alternative if you are really having a hard time figuring out what type of gaming hardware to buy or a great complementary gift to a larger gift as well.

8 Buy a gift card for your recipient's favourite game or electronics store. If you can't figure out what to buy, here's a sure-fire way to ensure your gamer gets what he or she wants.

9 Help your gamer enjoy their gaming experience in comfort. Beanbags and other chairs that are designed for gaming will be a huge hit with your recipient. For good measure, throw in their favourite snacks or beverages to enjoy while they play.

10 You don't have to follow the latest in gaming news to find the perfect gift. Since there are so many different gift options available, there are plenty of ways to enhance the playing experience for the gamer in your life.

Source: http://www.brandpointcontent.com/PrintSite/Article.aspx?ArticleId=16451

Test your understanding

1 Tick (✓) the correct answer. A *gamer* is someone who

a likes playing board games. ______

b enjoys playing video games. ______

c likes playing games with other people. ______

d creates video games. ______

2 Read paragraph 2. Why is there no such thing as a gamer who has everything?

____

____

____

3 Mark the following statements True (T) or False (F) according to the article.

a ______ If you aren't a gamer yourself, buying for a gamer can be difficult.

b ______ TRANSFORMERS PRIME is a game for adults only.

c ______ An extra controller is an example of an accessory.

d ______ It is a mistake to buy a gamer a gift card.

e ______ You need to follow the latest in gaming news in order to find the perfect gift.

4 Tick (✓) the correct answer. Paragraph 3 refers to game *genres*. Game genres refer to game

a characters. ______

b players. ______

c buyers. ______

d categories. ______

5 The following sentences are from the article. Tick (✓) two examples that use language that describes a game.

a You don't have to follow the latest in gaming news to find the perfect gift. ______

b Keep in mind that gamers are always looking for ways to improve their playing experience. ______

c The game is a cinematic and immersive action shooter available for PlayStation 3, Xbox 360 and PC. ______

d Help your gamer enjoy their gaming experience in comfort. ______

e TRANSFORMERS PRIME is a family-friendly game based on the popular animated television series of the same name. ______

6 Tick (✓) the correct answer. In paragraph 3, the word *classic* in 'Buy them new games based on fan-favourite classic brands' could be replaced by

a old-fashioned. ______

b traditional. ______

c well-known and popular. ______

d common. ______

7 Tick (✓) the correct answer. The purpose of paragraph 4 is to

a provide information on TRANSFORMERS: FALL OF CYBERTRON. ______

b persuade readers that they should buy TRANSFORMERS: FALL OF CYBERTRON. ______

c give advice on how to play TRANSFORMERS: FALL OF CYBERTRON. ______

d both a and b ______

e both a and c ______

8 Does the TRANSFORMERS game sound like a game you would be interested in playing? Why/Why not?

____

____

____

____

____

9 Use your dictionary to look up the meanings of the following **bold** words in each sentence.

a Do a little fishing for ideas by talking to your **recipient**.

Recipient means ______________________________

b … buying can sometimes be a bit overwhelming considering the rapidly **evolving** technology and the choices in video games.

Evolving means ______________________________

c Find a genre that features **inherently** fun and timelessly cool gameplay.

Inherently means ______________________________

d TRANSFORMERS: FALL OF CYBERTRON allows players to experience the most **pivotal**, post-apocalyptic battles of TRANSFORMERS **lore** that lead to their famed **exodus** from their home planet.

Pivotal means ______________________________

Lore means ______________________________

Exodus means ______________________________

10 The article offers a variety of advice for people looking to buy a gift for a gamer. Using information from the article, what do you think are the three most important things a person should do when looking for a gift for a gamer?

1 ______________________________

2 ______________________________

3 ______________________________

Boost your reading skills

Reading critically

The ability to read **critically** is an essential reading skill. Looking closely at language can help you decide what the writer's purpose or purposes are. It can help you 'read between the lines' and uncover ideas and information. It is also helpful to determine whether an author is **for** or **against** an idea.

1 When we say that we are 'for' an idea, what do we really mean? Underline the best three possible answers.

- **a** we *support* the idea
- **b** we *disagree with* the idea
- **c** we *back* the idea
- **d** we *are confused by* the idea
- **e** we *approve of* the idea

Look at the following example from the advice article.

> Great for younger fans, TRANSFORMERS PRIME is a family-friendly game based on the popular animated television series of the same name.

In this example, the author is clearly **for** the game. Three words that tell you this are: *great*, *family-friendly* and *popular*.

2 Now you try. Answer each of the following.

a With a few bits of good advice, you can easily find a gift that will delight anyone who enjoys gaming.

Is the author for or against finding a game as a gift? ______________

What words support your answer? ______________ and ______________

b Here are a few ways to find the perfect gift for the video game-lover in your life.

Is the author for or against finding a game as a gift? ______________

What words support your answer? ______________ and ______________

c Beanbags and other chairs that are designed for gaming will be a huge hit with your recipient.

Is the author for or against finding special gaming furniture? ______________

What words support your answer? ______________ and ______________

d … the game is a cinematic and immersive action shooter available for PlayStation 3, Xbox 360 and PC.

Is the author for or against the game TRANSFORMERS PRIME? ______________

What words support your answer? ______________ and ______________

3 Although the article has the overall purpose of giving advice about gifts for gamers, it also has other purposes. Look at each example from the article. Mark each with one of the following choices:

- **promote** to show whether the author is promoting (endorsing) a game—the language will be *persuasive* and make the game sound really great and desirable
- **advice** if you think the author is offering advice—the language will be helpful and contain verbs of instruction, such as *get* and *buy*
- **information** if you think the sentence is informative.

The first one has been done for you.

a Buy a gift card for your recipient's favourite game or electronics store. advice

b This holiday season, you can find two new offerings from the TRANSFORMERS franchise for gamers of every age. ______________

c For good measure, throw in their favourite snacks or beverages to enjoy while they play. ______________

d TRANSFORMERS: FALL OF CYBERTRON allows players to experience the most pivotal, post-apocalyptic battles of TRANSFORMERS lore. ______________

e Great for older teens and adults, the game is a cinematic and immersive action shooter available for PlayStation 3. ______________

Work on words

Root words and prefixes

A **root** is the **basic form** of a word, and is the foundation on which the meaning of other words can be built. Whenever you come upon an unfamiliar word, it can be helpful to see if you recognise its root. Even if you can't define a word exactly, recognising the root gives you a general idea of the word's meaning.

Look at the following examples. The root word (smallest possible word) has been identified for you.

Word	Root (smallest form) of word
aquarium	*aqua* (water)
audible	*audio* (sound)
geography	*geo* (earth)
thermometer	*thermo* (heat)

1 Look at the following list of words. Write the **root** word.

a sickness ______________

b motherly ______________

c ventilate ______________

d freedom ____________

e unbaked ____________

f reviewed ____________

g dictation ____________

h minimal ____________

Adding prefixes

A **prefix** is a letter or group of letters attached to the beginning of a word that changes the word's meaning.

For example: the word *significant* means 'important, worthy or great'. With the prefix *in*, the word becomes *insignificant*, which then means 'the opposite of significant—unimportant, irrelevant or minor'.

Examples of adding a prefix to a root:

tele + phone → telephone (to speak from afar)

anti + social → antisocial (disruptive or offensive behaviour)

2 Add a **prefix** to these **root** words to fill in the gaps.

My friends and I often ____________(agree) on the best books to read. They often ____________(like) my suggestions, and I may have to ____________(consider) the books I suggest. I don't want them to be ____________(happy) with my suggestions. I hope to ____________(cover) what books they like!

3 Guess the meanings of the following **prefixes** by looking at the words they create.

Prefix	Word 1	Word 2	Prefix meaning?
bi	bicycle	biannual	two or twice
re	re-enter	relist	
inter	interact	interchange	
dis	dislike	displease	
mis	misunderstand	misbehaviour	
astro	astronaut	astronomer	

4 The second column below contains **root** words from the article. Match them to a **prefix** from the first column to create a new word. Then write the definition of the new word beside it. Use a dictionary if you need to.

Prefix	Root word	New word	Definition
inter	allow	interplay	relationship, interaction
re	official		
un	human		
dis	play		
sub	design		

Spotlight on language

The language of giving advice

One of the article's purposes is to **give advice** on buying gifts for gamers. In order to give advice, the author uses language that tells you what to do, but in a polite way.

An **imperative verb** delivers a request, gives a command, or states a desire or wish. Typically, imperative sentences are short and simple, but they can be longer as well. Some of the simplest sentences in the English language are actually imperative sentences consisting of a single verb.

For example: Stop! Go. Hurry!

Imperative verbs are also known as 'bossy verbs' because they tell people what to do.

For example: **Shut** the door, **finish** your meal and **listen** to me.

1 Imperative sentences often begin with **verbs** (action words). Look at the following examples from the article and underline the **imperative verbs**. Some sentences may have more than one. The first one has been done for you.

- **a** Think about accessories.
- **b** Keep in mind that gamers are always looking for ways to improve their playing experience.
- **c** Do a little fishing for ideas by talking to your recipient (or his or her parents) and see if there's something special to add to their gaming setup.
- **d** Find official apparel from their favourite game titles or vintage video game T-shirts, which are sure to be a hit ...
- **e** Buy a gift card for your recipient's favourite game or electronics store.
- **f** Help your gamer enjoy their gaming experience in comfort. Beanbags and other chairs that are designed for gaming will be a huge hit with your recipient. For good measure, throw in their favourite snacks or beverages to enjoy while they play.

2 Do you think the author of the article is being 'bossy' by using all these **imperative verbs**?

____

Why/Why not?

____

____

____

____

3 Imperative verbs give instructions by giving advice and telling people what to do. Can you think of other situations where **imperative verbs** are used?

____

____

____

____

Extend your skills

Think about a product that you know a lot about (e.g. a game, smartphone or book). Choose one and write an email to a friend about the product, giving advice on what you know and making some suggestions for them.

Answers

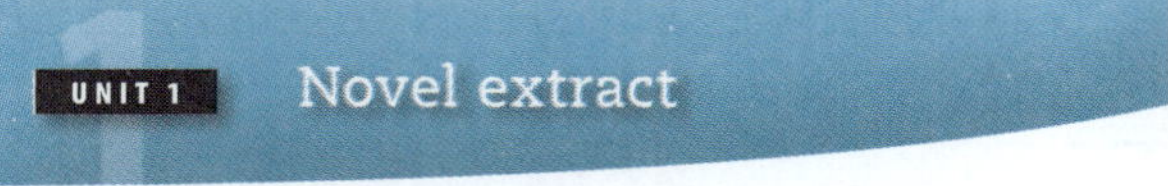

UNIT 1 Novel extract

Before you read pages 2–3

1 girl

2 the country

3 adventure

Test your understanding pages 3–4

1 **a** T **b** F **c** F **d** T **e** T **f** F

2 **a** 3 **b** 5 **c** 1 **d** 2 **e** 4

3 c

4 b

5 c

6 Answers will vary.

Boost your reading skills pages 4–5

1
- **a** The 'shadow' allows us to infer that Lena did not appreciate or like the present she was opening.
- **b** 'I wouldn't eat on that table after that two year old if I were you' infers that the table is probably dirty and messy after the child sat there.
- **c** Simon probably did something wrong and is being punished.
- **d** The day was hot and the heat melted the ice-cream.
- **e** There had been an accident somewhere and the ambulance was speeding to get there.

2
- **a** The men are not known to Dot as they speak to her so strangely and she does not know their names.
- **b** The men look *terrible* to Dot in that they are big, scary and strange.
- **c** The men attempt to make their voices *small* to Dot as they are trying not to frighten her; however, she is still not comforted by their presence.
- **d** The men are *more sad and less noisy* as they still have not found the lost child. They are giving up hope of finding him alive.
- **e** The little boy has been found, but he has died in the bush.
- **f** Dot feels terribly scared and upset by the memory of the other child and by what this means for her safety. She worries about what effect her absence is having on her parents ('These thoughts made her so miserable that she began to cry herself.').

Work on words pages 5–7

1
- **c** little, dry, bare, straggly, prickly
- **d** The landscape is dry and sparse. There are many trees, bushes and shrubs that Dot has to push through.
- **e** little
- **f** The adjective 'little' makes Dot appear small and vulnerable and reinforces the danger of her situation.
- **g** tall, far-off, crooked
- **h** The height of the trees are exaggerated to make Dot appear little and defenceless.
- **i** little, blue, tangled, drooping
- **j** Dot would feel isolated and disoriented at only being able to see 'little patches of blue sky'.

2 The setting's description provides a sense of the harshness of Dot's location. The descriptions of the largeness and harshness of nature contrast sharply with Dot's smallness and innocence. This works to create tension and fear for her situation.

3
- **a** severe
- **b** enormous
- **c** stark

4 **a** dry: dehydrated/parched/waterless. scraggy: scrawny/lean/thin

b cruel: punishing/harsh/forbidding. wild: desolate/barren/harsh

5 Answers will vary. Dot is small and innocent. She is physically contrasted by her harsh environment. She tells the story from her perspective—that of a young girl. The reader is moved to be concerned about her safety.

Spotlight on language pages 7–8

1 **a** TP **b** FP **c** TP **d** FP **e** FP **f** TP

2 **b** It seemed such a long, long time since my mother had told me that I might gather some bush flowers while she cooked the dinner.

c I wondered now if all these rough, big men were riding into the bush to find me, and if, after many days, they would find me and no one ever see me again.

d I seemed to see my mother crying, and my father very sad, and all the men very solemn.

e It seemed a long time before I summoned up courage to uncover my weeping eyes, and look once more at the bare, dry earth.

Extend your skills page 9

Answers will vary. Some stylistic areas that should match the original include the following:

- the correct narrative perspective (first, second, third person etc.)
- simple descriptive language
- past tense.

You might like to introduce some dialogue (conversation) now that a new character has appeared.

UNIT 2 Web article

Before you read pages 10–11

1 26 January

2 Answers will vary.

3 Australians overseas may like to have a lunch or visit other Australians. They might do things that remind them of home, like have a barbeque or play some sport. They might call their family in Australia.

Test your understanding pages 11–12

1 **a** T **b** T **c** F **d** F **e** T **f** T

2 b

3 b

4 Answers will vary. At least three whole paragraphs contain information about celebrating with food.

5 c

6 a

7 d

8 Answers will vary. This is an expression used to show that despite not having or using a barbeque to cook meat, you can still create an authentic barbeque experience.

Boost your reading skills pages 13–14

1 Answers will vary. The main idea is the most important thing the paragraph says about the topic. It is the overall idea of a paragraph.

2 **a** People who are Australians or who are interested in Australia and who would like to celebrate Australia Day, even if they are overseas.

b Ways to celebrate Australia Day if you live in the Northern Hemisphere.

c People who live outside of Australia, particularly in the Northern Hemisphere.

d January 8, 2006

e The article was written to encourage Australians and non-Australians to get together and celebrate Australia Day.

3 Even if you aren't in Australia, you could throw an 'Australia Day' party. Celebrating with many different people shows the true meaning of 'mateship'.

4 **b** Possible highlighted words: authentic, local, activities, together, learn, fun. Possible paragraph title: Finding local activities

c Possible highlighted words: dessert, close, variety, less traditional. Possible paragraph title: Dessert ideas

Work on words pages 14–16

1 **a** aren't

i aunt **ii** aren't **iii** aren't, aunt

b your

i you're **ii** your **iii** your, you're

c complement

i compliment **ii** complement
iii compliment, complement

d flair

i flair **ii** flare **iii** flair, flare

e angel, sweets, choose

i angle **ii** angel **iii** sweets **iv** suites
v chews **vi** choose

2 **a** i desert **ii** dessert **iii** desert
iv desert, dessert

b i allowed **ii** aloud **iii** allowed, aloud

c i bare **ii** bear **iii** bear **iv** bare
v bear, bare

3 Answers will vary.

Spotlight on language pages 17–18

1

bad	abrasive
natural	feeling
numb	luck
mild	order
fairly	fun
random	giant
serious	dark
little	aware
vaguely	additives

2 **b** 'Gentlemen, I want you to know that I am not always right, but I am never wrong.'

c Honk if you're against noise pollution!

d 'I'll give you a definite maybe.'

e 'I am a deeply superficial person.'

f I'm proud of my humility.

g 'If I could drop dead right now, I'd be the happiest man alive!'

h 'If you fall and break your legs, don't come running to me.'

i 'Parting is such sweet sorrow.'

j 'I distinctly remember forgetting that.'

3 **a** In order to stand you need to be up, not down.

b A story is made up and therefore not true.

c How can something that is tight also be loose?

d 'Taped' implies that it will be shown later and not be 'live'.

e To gamble is never sure or certain.

Extend your skills page 19

Answers will vary. Some stylistic areas present in blog comments include the following:

* an informal style that is conversational
* personal language of opinion: *I think, I believe, I hope*
* present tense: *I am.*

You might like to respond to some of the ideas of the blog comment already posted.

UNIT 3 Website advertisement

Before you read pages 20–21

1 Answers will vary.

2 Answers will vary. Some answers may support or not support the idea of a gymnastics class for young children.

Test your understanding pages 21–22

1 **a** T **b** F **c** F **d** T **e** F **f** T

2 d

3 c

4 d

5 Answers will vary. 'Carer participation' implies that parents and carers will get involved in the class and have an active role in supporting their child in the activities.

6 c

7 d

8 Answers will vary. The colours blue and orange are bright and appealing colours that suit the 'fun' nature of the classes being advertised. They are colours that are not identified with any gender, making the ad appeal to both boys and girls. Colour creates a cohesive tie or a colour thematic link that connects all parts of the advertisement together.

9 a

10 b

11 Answers will vary.

Boost your reading skills pages 23–24

1
- **a** recipes
- **b** textbooks
- **c** short stories/films
- **d** biography/autobiography
- **e** movie poster/book review
- **f** business/personal letters
- **g** community announcements

2
- **a** persuade
- **b** instruct
- **c** entertain
- **d** recount
- **e** raise awareness
- **f** inform

3

Language that persuades	**Language that informs**
bright colours	Tumble Bears are able to extend their core gymnastics skills
gymnastics is a fun, engaging approach	Tumble Tigers classes are more structured and carried out without carers.
NEW Fantastic gymnastics!	Tumble Bugs are our beginner 2-3 year olds.

4 Persuasive language: vital for healthy lives, fun songs, encouraging independence and self-confidence

Informative language: Classes are non-competitive and age-specific, Tumble Bears are able to extend their core gymnastics skills

Work on words pages 24–25

1

collaborate	connect, link, associate
compress	behave with sympathy and kindness
correlate	gather together as a group or flock
congregate	cooperate, work together
compassion	press down on, to press together

2
- **a** coordination: dexterous, agile, deft
- **b** competitive: ambitious, combative
- **c** confidence: assurance, poise

3 **a**

i prognosis	passage before the main part
ii propel	prediction of what will happen; diagnosis
iii prophet	to act before, in advance
iv prologue	person who foretells the future
v proactive	forward motion

b Answers will vary. The word *progress* means 'growth, advancement and improvement'. This connects in meaning to the Latin *pro* meaning 'forward', which is what you do when you *progress*.

4

a far, distant	unpopular, unkind, unhappy, unlucky
b eight	biweekly, bimonthly, biannual
c badly, wrong, incorrect	delete, deforestation, decentralise, decongest
d remove, take away, get rid of	television, telephone, telescope, telecommunication
e not (opposite of something)	reply, repeat, resend, restart, reboot, remember
f again, once more or back	preview, predict, prehistoric, prefix, preparation
g twice	octopus, octave, octogenarian, October
h one, whole, same	uniform, unify
i before	subway, submarine, subtract, subdue, subordinates
j under or low	mistake, misunderstand, misbehave, misread, miscalculate
k many or more than two	multiple, multiply, multicoloured, multilingual

Spotlight on language pages 26–27

1 Answers will vary. Some suggestions are:

- **b** tastier
- **c** cleaner/fresher
- **d** healthier
- **e** stylish

2 **b** ✗ **c** ✓ **d** ✓ **e** ✗ **f** ✗

Extend your skills page 27

Answers will vary. Layout: the logo is placed in the top left-hand corner and is the first thing the reader sees. Large font is used for the heading 'CALL TO BOOK' to encourage potential customers to make a booking. This is followed by a further stylised font 'NEW Fantastic gymnastics' that is eye catching, easy to read and draws the reader's eye down towards more detailed product information. The information is paragraphed under subheadings that are easy to follow.

Language: use of jargon related to the subject of gymnastics makes the information appear reliable and authentic. Persuasive language is used to highlight the benefits of the activity.

Graphics: three action shots of children in different gymnastic positions reinforce the activity being advertised. The action shot of the trampoline and jumper grabs the reader's attention and creates a sense of action and activity. The trampoline in the logo creates a visual tie to the trampoline in the photograph.

UNIT 4 Interview

Before you read pages 28–29

1 c

Test your understanding pages 30–31

1 **a** T **b** F **c** T **d** T **e** F

2 a

3 c

4 c

5 a and b

6 Answers will vary. Terry's main message is that in order to be a good reader yourself, you need to read a wide variety of books. In addition, you should avoid the style of the book you are trying to write as it may restrict your ideas. Also, you need to start paying attention to spelling, punctuation and grammar.

7 c

8 d

9 Answers will vary. Different readers may enjoy an exciting storyline, or different and unusual settings. They may like stories about people and relationships, or stories that are funny.

10 b

11 Answers will vary. Some readers may enjoy fantasy novels, which is the genre (category) of story that Terry writes. Others may not like this style and prefer books about animals or friendships.

12 Answers will vary.

Boost your reading skills page 32

1 **a** O **b** E **c** M **d** M **e** O **f** E **g** O **h** M **i** E **j** M

Work on words pages 32–34

1

- **a** Terry is saying that if you 'get this right' (reading about the world and reading everything you can) then writing will be 'a piece of cake'—meaning it will be easy and no great hardship.
- **b** 'Screwed up' is an informal way of talking about people who are messed up, who have problems and are not 'normal'. People like to read about these characters as they are more interesting.
- **c** A 'holy grail' is a metaphor for something that is highly sought after. Terry is saying here that there is no secret to being a good writer and that being a good writer does not just magically happen. You can work hard at it to achieve success.
- **d** Again, like the 'holy grail' example, Terry is trying to explain that through perseverance and hard work anyone could be a good writer. It does not just magically occur.
- **e** ii and iv

2

a	Although she went to court, she was only given a slap on the wrist.	there was no better
b	Wow! This dress costs an arm and a leg.	a mild punishment
c	She was tickled pink by the present.	it is extremely expensive
d	We're all in the same boat.	not healthy
e	That was hands down the best dinner I've eaten all year.	made very glad
f	He's a bit of a loose cannon.	all of us are in the same position
g	That show is driving me up the wall!	unpredictable
h	I've been feeling under the weather.	making me very irritated

3
- **a** let's get started/let's get to work/let's begin
- **b** not young any more
- **c** poor/have no money at the moment
- **d** to share/tell something
- **e** ripped off/taken advantage of
- **f** someone cherished/valued above others (precious)
- **g** spot on/you got it right/you are correct

Spotlight on language pages 34–35

1 Um, Oh

2 In section 3, the sentence that shows Terry's pause is '… she's another one … and they all make interesting people …'

3 fantasy, parody, characters, author, series, manuscript, spelling, punctuation, grammar

4 'Can anyone tell me what *it's* all about …?'

5 Examples include: 'It's like *Lord of the Rings*'—this is an example of a simile and is often used in informal situations. 'Especially a very popular character!'—this is an example of a short, incomplete sentence. 'the nice characters aren't that fun'—this sentence contains a contraction (aren't) as well as the informal word 'fun'.

Extend your skills pages 36–37

Answers will vary. Questions written should be suitable for their location within the interview (e.g. Question 1: beginning of interview).

So, how long have you been writing for?

Ah, it feels like forever! No, seriously, I started writing when I was in primary school. I would create these really weird characters … well, everyone else thought they were weird!

UNIT 5 Information text

Before you read pages 38–39

1 Answers will vary. All the images appear to have a group of people with one other stand-out person present who may be a leader or director. The stand-out character may be communicating ideas such as being an individual, being different or standing out from the crowd. The images may have something to do with management, leadership, team work, team leaders, success through team work or successful teams requiring a strong team leader.

2 Answers will vary. Key words and ideas should be nouns (people, places or things) associated with the topic and not words such as *the, it* or *he.* Possible key words/ideas from the article include: *team leader, guidance, leadership, goals, listens, responsibilities, motivate* and *responsibility*.

Test your understanding pages 39–41

1
- **a** stand out from the crowd
- **b** team leader
- **c** team strategy (the chess board is a clue to the idea of 'strategy')

2 a

3 a

4

a leader	the people who make up the group/team
b guidance	involving shared participation in working towards a common goal
c key result	a person who offers direction and assistance
d cooperative	a main/significant outcome
e team	assistance/supervision/leadership

5 d

6 Answers will vary. Section 5 states that a team leader is someone who cooperates with their team. The key word 'contrasts' indicates to the reader that the 'commander' is different from the team leader. A commander would be a leader who gives orders rather than listens to and works with the team.

7 b

8
- **b** motivate
- **c** responsibility
- **d** persevering
- **e** flexible
- **f** initiative

9 Answers will vary. The newsletter is focusing on an important leadership skill—team leading—in order to communicate that in leadership situations students are often required to motivate and lead each other, as well as work effectively as a team. These are skills that are also needed in adulthood in the workforce.

Boost your reading skills pages 41–42

Source: The source of the information is the *Wombat High Newsletter* Issue 11 from October.	
1 Team leader (section 1)	A team leader or team lead is someone who offers assistance and direction. They provide this for their team and they are all responsible for working together to achieve a work outcome.
4 Leadership involves (section 5)	Leadership involves a variety of skills including offering guidance and being accountable, organised, purposeful, determined, accepting and open minded.
3 Features of a good team leader (section 2)	A team leader is someone students look to for support and direction when working together to solve a problem.

Comments:

Answers will vary. You may have questions about the article that you need to research or ask an adult about.

Work on words pages 42–44

1
- **a** contentment
- **b** malicious
- **c** vulnerable
- **d** common
- **e** hesitant

2 **b** S **c** S **d** S **e** S **f** A **g** A **h** S
i A **j** A **k** A **l** S

3
- **a** leader: head, frontrunner, manager, superior
  guidance: direction, assistance, leadership
- **b** good: worthy, commendable, praise-worthy, creditable
  achieve: attain, complete, succeed
- **c** trust: belief, confidence, dependence
- **d** opportunity: chance, prospect
  influence: impact, affect, inspire
- **e** connect: join, link, unite
  succeed: flourish, thrive, prosper

4
- **b** ingenuity, resourcefulness
- **c** goal, aim
- **d** determined, purposeful
- **e** accountability, duty
- **f** bendable, malleable

Spotlight on language pages 44–45

1
- **b** The politician was reserved and unpopular with his voters.
- **c** The newsreader had an engaging way of speaking.
- **d** The behaviour of the students was not at all impressive.
- **e** The new team leader was meticulous and thorough.

2
- **a** ~~I believe~~ a ~~cool~~ team leader is a person ~~like you~~ who provides guidance,

instruction, direction and leadership to a group of other individuals.

b ~~We don't think~~ the team members should directly report or answer to the team leader but ~~we think~~ they should be expected to provide support to the team leader in achieving the group's ~~brilliant~~ goals.

3 **b** team leader, constructively, goals

c team leader, cooperative, team, typical command structure

UNIT 6 Reading Shakespeare

Before you read pages 48–49

1 Enmity means hostility, hate, antagonism. Other words and ideas from paragraph 1 that support the idea that the families are feuding include quarrel, bloodshed, fierce, brawls and disturbed.

2 b

Test your understanding pages 49–50

1

Capulets and Montagues	Romeo's close friend
Romeo	a girl whom Romeo is infatuated with, but who does not return his love
Benvolio	the head and leader of the Capulet family
Rosaline	son of the old Lord Montague
Old Lord Capulet	wealthy feuding families of Verona

2 **a** 5 **b** 4 **c** 2 **d** 1 **e** 3

3 c

4 a

5 Answers will vary. That Old Capulet 'could have told a whispering tale in a fair lady's ear' reveals that as a young man he was good looking, charming and popular with young ladies.

6 **a** Answers will vary. You could argue that Romeo is *sincere* as he appears to honestly love Rosaline, *playful* as he agrees to attend the party in disguise or *senseless* as he forgets Rosaline very quickly once he sees Juliet. He also places himself and his family in danger by attending the party.

b Answers will vary. You could argue that Benvolio is a *risk-taker* as he attends the Capulets party, *genuine* as he seems honestly interested in his friend Romeo or a *troublemaker* as he deliberately leads Romeo into a dangerous situation.

c Answers will vary. You could argue that the feud between the families is *pointless* as it has been going on for so long, *honourable* as family members take the feud so seriously or *necessary* as the violence being committed against each family should not be ignored.

Boost your reading skills pages 50–51

1 **b** variety

c affected by

d radiate

e interrupted

2 **a** masked/camouflaged/covered

b not diseased/not afflicted

c evicted/expelled/ejected

d informal/unendorsed

e unexpected/unanticipated

f different/distinct

Work on words page 52

1 **b** resulted/followed

c did not belong to/originate from the house of Montague

d Rosaline never returned Romeo's love

e began/started

2 **a** chief

b brawl

c fair

d courtesy

Spotlight on language pages 53–54

1 **a** S

b Juliet

- **c** the other ladies
- **d** the image of Juliet being white and pure like a 'snowy dove'

2
- **a** S
- **b** Juliet's beauty
- **c** the image of an exotic dark-skinned woman wearing a glistening jewel (The dark skinned woman is symbolic of night-time, which is the time Romeo lays eyes on Juliet. In his opinion, she 'glistens', sparkles and shines.)

3
- **a** M
- **b** Romeo
- **c** positive—Swans are associated with purity and beauty.
- **d** Benvolio
- **e** negative—a crow is a dirty, common and undesirable bird

Extend your skills page 54

1 **b** 5 **c** 3 **d** 4 **e** 2 **f** 6

UNIT 7 Picture book

Before you read pages 56–57

1 Answers will vary. Possums are generally shy, cautious and nervous. They are an indigenous (native) species.

2 Answers will vary. Rabbits are generally resourceful and multiply quickly. They are an introduced species that can quickly take over.

3 Answers will vary. You may notice the large painting in the centre. You may see the different types of animals presented and notice that some of them are wearing clothes. You may notice that some of the buildings are crumbling and destroyed.

Test your understanding pages 57–59

1 a

2 c

3 c

4 b

5 The story is told from the perspective (point of view) of the possums. I think this because the text states 'They didn't live in the trees, like we did'. The image shows the possums living in the trees.

6 Answers will vary.

7 white coloured, long ears, tails

8 standing up, wearing uniforms, pointing, looking stern, wearing eyeglasses

9 Answers will vary.

Possums	Both	Rabbits
Equal	Both are animals	Dominant
Grouped together	Share the setting	Status
Possums		Wearing clothes
Natural/ isolated/		Stern Forceful
In the trees		Rabbits
Outsiders		Appear human

10 c

11 Answers will vary.

12 d

13 Answers will vary. The picture book contains ideas that would appeal to both a young and older audience. The images are imaginative and interesting and would appeal to children. The story is on one level simple, however contains deeper themes and ideas that would interest an adult audience.

14 Answers will vary.

15 c

Boost your reading skills pages 59–61

1

a	the top of page	the painting
b	the foreground (centre front)	the collapsing buildings
c	the mid-ground (middle)	two rabbits
d	featured in the background	the possums

2 b

3 curious, natural, conversational, watchful

4 stiff, purposeful, upright, ordered

5 **a** The rabbits are wearing an old fashioned military uniform with detailed stitching and accessories. The colours are stark and strong. They wear objects like eyeglasses.

b The possums are natural and indigenous to the land they occupy. They do not wear clothes and have not acquired 'things' in the same way the rabbits have. They both represent different value systems.

c The rabbits appear more powerful as there is an aggression about them, due in part to their military attire and body language. The possums are isolated and separate.

Work on words pages 61–63

1
- **a** ladies' restroom
- **b** men's restroom
- **c** wheelchair access
- **d** turn left
- **e** turn right
- **f** surveillance
- **g** airport/aeroplane
- **h** rubbish/waste
- **i** post office/post box
- **j** baby-feeding room
- **k** restaurant
- **l** café
- **m** fast food

2

Symbol	Possible meaning/s
	love, romance, relationships, valentine, femininity
✓	approval, support, correct
	danger, poison, hazard, risk, peril, menace
	disapproval, displeasure, dissatisfaction
	time, urgency, deadline, time limit
	escape, possibility, opportunity, risk, chance, error
	courage, danger, stealth, bravery

3

Item/ character	What they symbolise	What the symbol further suggests
possums	native species, indigenous	natural, unprotected, innocent
rabbits	invaders, colonisers	aggressors, trespassers, intruders,
rabbits' clothes	uniform	military, war, aggression, hostility, conflict, threat
wheel	technology	skill, knowledge, machinery, tools, civilisation, organisation
clock	time	order, calendar, deadlines, business
tree	nature	natural habitat, environment
eyeglass	technology/ education	education, advancement, knowledge, information, scrutiny, inspection, examination

Spotlight on language pages 63–64

1 (the painting)

2 Answers may vary; however, you should notice the rabbits, the buildings and lastly the possums in the top corner.

3 Answers will vary. The possums have been placed in the top corner as they are alone and powerless. It is the rabbits who dominate the environment, and their placement conveys this.

4 The space the rabbits occupy is divided from the space the possums occupy. This vector highlights the differences between the two groups.

5 **a** outwards, inwards at the painting

b no

c no

d The rabbits are militaristic in their posture and attitude. They have a 'trained' look that is contrasted by the possums' naturalness.

6 **a** towards each other, inwards, towards the rabbits

b yes

c The rabbits are building a new place for themselves that does not include the possums. The possums live in different houses.

d The rabbits and possums are different, but the rabbits are the ones who maintain the control and power in their relationship.

Extend your skills page 65

1 Answers will vary.

2 Answers will vary.

UNIT 8 Novel extract

Before you read pages 66–67

Answers will vary. Students may have knowledge of the white rabbit, Alice, the rabbit-hole, the Cheshire cat, the Queen of Hearts, Alice growing small, Alice growing large, magic cake, magic drink, 'Eat me' or 'Drink me'.

Test your understanding pages 67–69

1 a

2 Answers will vary. The story begins with Alice sitting under a tree when something interesting happens—the White Rabbit runs by. This is unlikely to occur during the middle or end of a story.

3 **a** 2 **b** 4 **c** 1 **d** 5 **e** 3

4 Answers will vary. Alice is an imaginative and creative girl who loves stories, particularly stories with pictures as they spark her imagination, but not stories that are long or that would be read during school.

5 a

6 b

7 Answers will vary. Alice behaves with spontaneity—she is impulsive and acts without thought as she is desperate for adventure.

8 c

9 d

10 d

11 b

12 c

13 Answers will vary. Students may think Alice is impulsive and a risk-taker, some might admire her spirited personality or some may think she is behaving with dangerous thoughtlessness.

Boost your reading skills pages 69–70

1 **b** If I leave for work at 8 am, I can usually walk to the beach early in the morning.

c Although it was extremely expensive, Clarice bought the bag anyway.

d Whenever Harry goes to the cinema he enjoys going with his friend Paul.

e I prefer to watch TV over the Internet as it allows me to watch what I want when I want.

f If it looks like we are going to have heavy rain, I have to bring in the washing straight away.

2 **a** 'Alice started to her feet, for it flashed across her mind that she had never before seen a rabbit with either a waistcoat-pocket, or a watch to take out of it…'

b 'In another moment down went Alice after it, never once considering how in the world she was to get out again.'

c Why, I wouldn't say anything about it, even if I fell off the top of the house!'

3 'I wonder if I shall fall right *THROUGH* the earth! / How funny it'll seem to come out among the people that walk with their heads downward! / The Antipathies, I think—' / (she was rather glad there was no one listening, / this time, / as it didn't sound at all the right word) / '—but I shall have to ask them what the name of the country is, / you know. / Please, Ma'am, / is this New Zealand or Australia?' / (and she tried to curtsey as she spoke— / fancy *CURTSEYING* as you're falling through the air! / Do you think you could manage it?) / 'And what an ignorant little girl she'll think me for asking! / No, it'll never do to ask: / perhaps I shall see it written up somewhere.'

Work on words page 71

1 **b** often **c** so **d** there **e** rarely
f anywhere **g** surprisingly

2
a down
b straight, suddenly
c actually, on
d right, THROUGH
e very, very slowly, down

Spotlight on language pages 71–73

1 **b** was **c** is/was **d** wanted
e needed to buy

2
b should
c had
d should fall right through the earth
e should see it written up somewhere
f should have to ask them what the name of the country is

Extend your skills page 73

Answers will vary. Students may use a modern city setting and have Alice use modern technologies like a tablet, computer or mobile phone. Alice should use more modern informal language and colloquialisms and her sentences may not be as complex.

UNIT 9 Cartoons

Before you read pages 74–75

Answers will vary. Readers may note the main character is a businessman and the setting begins in an office before moving out to outer space.

Test your understanding pages 75–76

1 b

2 b

3 Answers will vary.

4 b

5 Answers will vary.

6 c

7 c and d

8 smug, self-important, arrogant

9 Answers will vary. The businessman's words reveal his sense of self-importance. His attitude about himself is revealed through the repetition of 'really'. He appears to be congratulating himself and assuring himself of his superiority in 'Hey this is ok'.

10 c

11 Answers will vary. You may notice the contrast between the first image and the last image. This shows you how small and insignificant the businessman actually is in the 'big picture'. You may also notice that although the businessman feels 'really really important', the businesses next to him are actually larger.

Boost your reading skills pages 77–78

1 **a**

Positive	Neutral	Negative
delighted	formal	depressed
loving	questioning	fearful
hopeful	serious	sarcastic
pleasant	knowledgeable	annoyed
pleased	solemn	spiteful
excited		outraged
sympathetic		
cheerful		

b thoughtful, critical, questioning

2 a, c, e

3
a The environment needs protecting.
c Women can be leaders.
d It's ok for boys to cry.
e it's important to recycle.

4
a Australia
b place of business
c the present
d modern

Work on words pages 79–81

1 **b** speech bubbles
c costume
d caption
e dialogue
f pun
g caricature
h punctuation
i facial expressions
j exaggeration
k body language
l length of shot

2 and **3**

Words associated with pictures/ images	Words associated with language
doodles	caption
caricatures ✓	dialogue
facial expressions ✓	punctuation ✓
body language ✓	pun
costume ✓	exaggeration ✓
exaggeration ✓	thought bubbles ✓

4 A cartoon is a simple drawing that often uses **satire**. It may or may not contain a caption. A cartoonist's purpose is to **expose** issues in society and influence public opinion. The cartoonist's purpose may be to entertain us and make us laugh. Or, their purpose may be more serious, through their use of **irony**. They may be sending an important message such as a social or political comment or criticism. The cartoonist in the text above uses words and pictures to reveal her **sarcasm** towards big business. The cartoonist makes businesses appear **ridiculous** in order to give an **insight** into aspects of our modern society.

Spotlight on language pages 81–82

1 **a** CEO, Co, Pty Ltd, Bigco, thought bubble, glasses, suit, tie, desk, office, body language (arms folded), appearance—nose is large, words 'really really important'.

b Letters—CEO are large and exaggerated to highlight the importance of his position. The man's nose is exaggerated to indicate a hardness and sternness about his personality. The repetition of the man's words 'really really important' exaggerate his sense of self importance.

c i and iii

2 Row 1—close-up
Row 2—medium shot
Row 3—long shot
Row 4—extreme long shot

3 c

4 Image 1 is an example of the way things can be in life. Like many people, the businessman believes himself to be very important because of his job.

5 The extreme long shot communicates the truth that on the grand scale and in the big picture we are not as important or as indispensable (necessary) as we believe ourselves to be.

UNIT 10 Fact sheet

Before you read page 84

1 c

2 Answers will vary. The fact sheet looks as though it is written for kids and young people, but it is really written for adults to give them healthy food and lifestyle ideas for their children.

Test your understanding pages 85–86

1 **a** T **b** F **c** T **d** T **e** F **f** F **g** T

2 a

3 c

4 b

5 Answers will vary. Some young people don't like the taste or texture of fruit and vegies. Some young people are wary of food that is 'good' for you and don't like being nagged to eat it. They may not like the texture of the peel and it may be bothersome to peel or cut it up.

6 d

Boost your reading skills pages 86–88

1 **a** lifecycle of a butterfly, how we sleep, precipitation

b Answers will vary. The cycle graph shows how healthy eating and exercise is a cycle that never ends. It is the constant practice of lifestyle choices that result in a healthy lifestyle.

c Answers will vary.

d Answers will vary.

2 **a** 1 to 2 **b** ii **c i** F **ii** T **iii** T **iv** T

d Answers will vary.

e

Benefits of eating fruit and vegetables	Statistics about fruit and vegetables	Effects of TV on healthy eating habits
Fruit and vegies contain vitamins, minerals and fibre.	Sixty per cent of children do not eat enough fruit and vegies.	Excessive TV watching results in soft drink consumption.
Fruit and vegies help young people grow, live with energy and avoid illness.		Less fruit and vegies are eaten.

Work on words pages 88–89

1

Location	Jargon
School	HSC, gifted and talented, PDHPE, curriculum
Gardeners	irrigate, landscaping
Politicians	constitution, left wing, lower house, democracy
The Internet	CYA, BTW, LOL, mouse
Cafes	ground beans, soy mocha chino
Science	astronomy, microscope, test tube, elements
Football	back pass, attacker

2 vitamins, recommended daily amount, obese, heart disease, source, minerals, dietary fibre

3 **b** nutritious, nourishing

c enduring, long-lasting

d pure, unprocessed

e oversupply, surplus

f inclination, craving

Spotlight on language pages 89–90

1 d

2

Does the instruction in the fact sheet:	Yes (✓)	No (✓)	Example
✷ start with an aim or goal?	✓		Information under *How to help kids and teens eat more fruit and vegies* provides the purpose/objective for the following recipe ideas.
✷ provide a list of what tools are needed?		✓	
✷ provide information on *how* to do something? (method)	✓		be creative … such as raw, sliced, grated, microwaved, mashed or baked … For example, add chopped, grated or pureed vegies to pasta sauces
✷ include a diagram or picture?		✓	
✷ use clear and brief vocabulary?	✓		Keep a bowl of fresh fruit in the home
✷ use the present tense?	✓		*keep* the fruit bowl full and *have* diced fruit … in the fridge
✷ use action verbs (e.g. take, put or mix)?	✓		involve, select, keep, chop, make, add, snack
✷ organise information by using bullet points?	✓		

3 Answers will vary. Despite not having all the features of an instruction, the recipe ideas do use important features such as bullet points and action verbs to communicate how to make healthy recipes.

UNIT 11 Biography

Before you read pages 92–93

1 Answers will vary. You may know that David Beckham is an English soccer player. He is also well known for his 'pop-star', musician and fashion-icon wife Victoria and their life in the public eye. Davis Beckham is also well known for his distinctive looks and tattoos.

2 Answers will vary.

Test your understanding pages 93–95

1 c

2 d

3 d

4 b

5 b

6 **a** 2 **b** 5 **c** 1 **d** 3 **e** 4

7 **a** N **b** P **c** N **d** P **e** N

8 Answers will vary. You may find you learnt more about David Beckham. You may find that he is a successful and talented soccer player who has had ups and downs in his career.

Boost your reading skills pages 95–96

1
- **a** to do something that compensates for poor past performance or behaviour
- **b** detest or strongly dislike
- **c** to be in disarray, disordered, messy
- **d** blocked or congested
- **e** captivating, delightful, enthralling

2
- **b** but his performance still needed
  Fine-tuning means refining or improving.
- **c** a few rough moments
  Notable means outstanding, remarkable, important.
- **d** responded with a swing towards the player
  Taunted means to be provoked and antagonised.
- **e** losing the match
  Knocked-out means to exit the competition as you have lost.
- **f** put him against the wall and fired up
  Poisonous means venomous, malicious, mean, nasty.

Work on words pages 96–97

1

a young	risk-taking
b brave	common
c thrifty	naive
d eccentric	old-fashioned
e famous	stingy
f popular	notorious
g antique	weird

2 The author's attitude towards David Beckham is mostly positive, complimentary and admiring.

3
- **a** ruthlessness
- **b** problematic
- **c** undeveloped, notorious
- **d** infamous, celebrity, vanity

Spotlight on language pages 97–98

1 **a** O **b** O **c** F **d** O **e** F **f** F

2
- **b** Every teenager has the right to learn to drive. O
- **c** The cost of living is increasing. F
- **d** Green is a relaxing colour. O
- **e** Tasmania is a lovely holiday destination. O

3 **a** F **b** O **c** O **d** O **e** O **f** F

UNIT 12 Advice article

Before you read pages 100–101

1 Answers will vary. Perhaps a friend needed some advice on buying a gift. You may have been asked advice on a topic you know well, like what games you are playing or what books you are reading.

2 Answers will vary. Key words in the opening paragraph like *gift, gamer, advice, holiday* and *season* tell us that the article will be giving advice on what gifts to give video gamers over the holiday season.

Test your understanding pages 101–103

1 b

2 Gamers are always looking for ways to improve their gaming experience.

3 **a** T **b** F **c** T **d** F **e** F

4 d

5 c and e

6 c

7 d

8 Answers will vary.

9 **a** receiver, beneficiary
b developing, growing, changing
c naturally, essentially, integrally
d focal, essential, crucial
e wisdom, legends, beliefs
f departure, exit, evacuation

10 Answers will vary but should contain examples from the article such as buy a gift card, or focus on accessories.

Boost your reading skills pages 103–104

1 **e** *support* the idea, we *back* the idea, we *approve* of the idea

2 **a** for: good, delight, enjoys
b for: perfect, game-lover
c for: huge, hit
d for: cinematic, immersive

3 **b** information
c advice
d promote
e promote

Work on words pages 104–105

1 **a** sick **b** mother **c** vent (wind) **d** free **e** bake **f** review **g** dict (say) **h** mini

2 My friends and I often **dis**(agree) on the best books to read. They often **dis**(like) my suggestions, and I may have to **re**(consider) the books I suggest. I don't want them to be **un**(happy) with my suggestions. I hope to **un**(cover) what books they like!

3

Prefix	Word 1	Word 2	Prefix meaning?
bi	bicycle	biannual	two or twice
re	re-enter	relist	**to do something again**
inter	interact	interchange	**between**
dis	dislike	displease	**not**
mis	misunderstand	misbehaviour	**not**
astro	astronaut	astronomer	**star**

4

Prefix	Root word	New word	Definition
inter	allow	interplay	relationship, interaction
re	official	**redesign**	**remake, do again**
un	human	**unofficial**	**informal, unauthorised**
dis	play	**disallow**	**forbid, ban**
sub	design	**subhuman**	**wicked, less than human**

Spotlight on language page 106

1

- **b** Keep in mind that gamers are always looking for ways to improve their playing experience.
- **c** Do a little fishing for ideas by talking to your recipient (or his or her parents) and see if there's something special to add to their gaming setup.
- **d** Find official apparel from their favourite game titles or vintage video game T-shirts, which are sure to be a hit.
- **e** Buy a gift card for your recipient's favourite game or electronics store.
- **f** Help your gamer enjoy their gaming experience in comfort. Beanbags and other chairs that are designed for gaming will be a huge hit with your recipient. For good measure, throw in their favourite snacks or beverages to enjoy while they play.

2 Answers will vary. The author is not being bossy, but is giving advice in a friendly and firm manner. This article is an example of how the imperative verb can be used in such a way that the reader does not feel commanded or ordered to do something.

3 Recipes, advertisements (Just do it!), 'how to' information, manuals.